"We Were One"

"We Were One"

Shoulder to Shoulder with the Marines Who Took Fallujah

PATRICK K. O'DONNELL

DA CAPO PRESS
A member of the Perseus Books Group

Library of Congress Cataloging-in-Publication Data is on file at the Library of Congress, Washington, D.C.

ISBN-10: 0-306-81469-2
ISBN-13: 978-0-306-81469-3

Published by Da Capo Press
A Member of the Perseus Books Group
http://www.dacapopress.com

Da Capo Press books are available at special discounts for bulk purchases in the U.S. by corporations, institutions, and other organizations. For more information, please contact the Special Markets Department at the Perseus Books Group, 11 Cambridge Center, Cambridge, MA 02142, or call (800)255-1514 or (617) 252-5298, or email special.markets@perseusbooks.com

1 2 3 4 5 6 7 8 9

This book is dedicated to America's fallen in the war in Iraq, and the Marines of 1st Platoon who gave their lives for a cause greater than themselves.
They fought with honor and for their brothers.
They are the next "Greatest Generation."

CONTENTS

CONTENTS

PREFACE

TEN MINUTES AFTER I HELPED DRAG A MORTALLY WOUNDED MARINE
out of a firefight, I was crouching in the courtyard of a nondescript
Fallujah house, watching two exhausted, grimy, visibly shaken
Marines gently load the bloodstained body into a Humvee. The
fallen man had been a close friend. Out of the blue, an angry gunnery sergeant confronted me: "Is this what you came here to see?"

"No," I responded.

"What are you going to write about here?"

"That I was with a band of heroes and I am going to tell the
truth about what happened here."

"Good. That's what these men deserve. People need to know
what happened here, their courage, and the sacrifices these men
made for each other and their country."

I volunteered to go to Iraq to become one of the first civilian his-
torians to accompany American men and women into combat, be
present as the action unfolded, and then write the history of their
war, allowing them to tell the story as much as possible in their own
words through oral history. I also went to Iraq to find out whether it
was true what several senior officers had told me, that our current
crop of young warriors is a remarkable group that deserves to be
called the next "Greatest Generation."

After spending several weeks in combat with U.S. Army and Marine special operations units, doing everything from conducting raids in Baghdad to inserting Special Operations teams, I joined the Third Battalion, First Marine Regiment, one of the infantry units mounting the frontal assault into the city of Fallujah. Through fate, or as one Marine captain described it, "It was meant to be," I was assigned to Lima Company's 1st Platoon, the unit that saw some the worst of the battle of Fallujah. After twelve days of house to house, hand to hand urban combat, only fourteen of the platoon's original complement of forty-six were still standing when Lima Company was withdrawn from the city.

First Platoon was more than just a fighting unit. The platoon was a closely knit family of men, best friends, who could and did lay down their lives for one another. The focus of this book is four pairs of best friends including the "heart and soul" of 1st Platoon—Lance Corporal Michael Hanks. Several of the more experienced men in the platoon didn't even have to be in Iraq; they selflessly extended their tours of duty so that they could protect the younger Marines who hadn't seen combat.

After the battle, the father of one of 1st Platoon's fallen Marines, with tears in his eyes, gripped my hand and said, "Tell my son's story." I leave it to the reader to decide whether, in telling this story, they are the next "Greatest Generation."

The world will little note nor long remember what we say here, but it can never forget what they did here . . . It is rather for us to be here dedicated to the great task remaining before us—that from these honored dead we take increased devotion to that cause for which they gave the last full measure of devotion.

—President Abraham Lincoln, The Gettysburg Address

PROLOGUE

OPERATION IRAQI FREEDOM I, SADR CITY, BAGHDAD, APRIL 2003: For Lance Corporal Michael Hanks and his best friend, Lance Corporal Bill Sojda, it was one more day in "paradise." Their nostrils were assaulted by an "ungodly" stench of rotting garbage and the putrid stream of raw sewage trickling in the gutter along the worn cobblestone street. Flies swarmed everywhere, in numbers so vast you could hear their wings beating, affixing themselves to sweaty upper lips until they were swatted away. The people were dirty. Even the women's faces were routinely smeared with dirt. Nearby, a young Iraqi child was swinging an IV bag full of bloody tissue. Thump! The child dropped the bag, spattering its gruesome contents all over the ground, making a bloody mess.

"This place is a hellhole," observed Hanks with his signature "George Bush-like" smirk. Hanks and Sojda had been inseparable since meeting two years earlier in the Marine School of the Infantry (SOI), a training school for basic combat skills attended by all recruits after boot camp.

The two Marines belonged to 1st Platoon, Lima Company, of the 3rd Battalion, 1st Marine Regiment. Battalion 3/1 spearheaded the initial invasion of Iraq in March 2003, fighting its way through the crossroads town of Nasiriyah into Baghdad, and ending up in Baghdad's worst ghetto, Sadr City. In the weeks following the capitulation of Baghdad, the Shiite Muslim neighborhood became a haven for criminals, the remnants of Saddam's army, and fanatical Islamist fighters from all over the Muslim world. For over a week, Hanks, Sojda and the rest of 3/1 had been patrolling the mean streets of Sadr City.

The Marines frequently encountered random potshots, and occasionally they faced full-scale ambushes. In one incident, the entire company was embroiled in a "hellacious" two-hour firefight. During the exchange, the barrels of their weapons grew white hot.

"Mount up," barked one of 1st Platoon's NCOs.

The men scrambled into three armored amphibious tracked vehicles, known variously as AAVs, amtracks, or tracks. Each track carried one of the platoon's three rifle squads. First Platoon's mission that day was routine: drop off medical supplies at a needy Iraqi clinic, pick up an informer who had intelligence on the enemy, and provide general security within Lima Company's area of operation.

Two Iraqi interpreters, one a woman, were accompanying the Marines. The "terps," often unarmed civilians, were needed to overcome the language barrier. Both translated this particular mission as an opportunity to get shot at. Sojda and Hanks brushed off the threat, claiming they enjoyed the adrenaline rush associated with combat.

Hanks, a burly, aggressive Marine, never missed an opportunity to get into a fight, either in a combat zone or in a bar. He always seemed to be in trouble, but at the same time, Hanks was a born leader who could get anyone to follow him, and would do anything to protect the people around him. He loved the Iraqi children, playing with them frequently, and handing out candy, water balloons, and squirt guns. Hanks loved to listen to himself talk. His sarcastic sense of humor, reminiscent of comedian Bill Murray, always seemed to keep everyone around him rolling with laughter.

In contrast, Bill Sojda, the quiet, decisive fire team leader, reminded people of Clint Eastwood. Sojda was a no-nonsense Marine, "known for not liking bullshit," and widely considered a "stud" on the battlefield. Both men were warriors. They didn't fear combat.

Hanks and Sojda trotted into the lead track, along with a third man they had met at the Marine School of the Infantry (SOI), Lance Corporal Benjamin Bryan. Fondly nicknamed "Opossum" because he was "kind of pudgy and short" and loved to munch on pizza and drink beer while off-duty in the barracks. In contrast to the other Marines, who tended to be very assertive, Bryan was very easy going and took life day by day. He was known as a "giver," someone who would give his friends the shirt off his back.

Gray smoke spewed from the tracks as they crunched through Baghdad's trash-strewn streets. After delivering the medical supplies, the Marines moved deeper into Sadr City to pick up the informer. After about twenty minutes, the tracks ground to a halt in front of one of the neighborhood's countless ramshackle apartment buildings. A four-man fire team hopped out of each track to provide security. Hank's, Sojda's, and Bryan's heads swiveled, looking for trouble, even as they skipped over the raw sewage pooling in the gutter.

As the Marines were about to clamber back into the tracks with the informant, "a massive explosion, bigger than any I've ever heard before, a nine on the Richter scale, shook the ground," remembered Sojda. Dust and debris flew through the air, as a massive mushroom cloud began to rise above a row of seedy apartment buildings several hundred meters away. Confusion reigned, as a stunned officer ordered the men first to mount, then to dismount, the tracks. *"What do you want us to do? Is the mission still on?"* thought Sojda. "Back in the tracks," barked an NCO. The Marines piled into the tracks and the armored column rumbled forward toward the source of the cloud. Sojda and Hanks drew "air security." They poked their heads out of the track's top hatch to watch for threats from above. After traveling about two hundred meters, the tracks began passing the bodies of blast victims lying in the street.

Nearly an entire block had been leveled by the blast. Terrorists had detonated an 18-wheeler loaded with crates of bullets, artillery shells, and at least one Scud missile. Both sides of the street were on fire, with burning ammunition thrown in every direction. As the tracks drew closer to the blaze, the Marines could see secondary explosions, as bullets and mortar rounds "cooked off" in a radius of about one hundred meters from the center of the explosion. Dead bodies littered the area. The tracks pulled up a couple of hundred meters from the blast crater, and the Marines dismounted.

Not much was left of the two-story houses in the neighborhood. Many had been reduced to rubble. Cars were flipped over up and down the street. One car had been hurled right through a building, creating a gaping hole in the building's façade. Fires raged throughout the buildings and palm tree fronds burned bright crimson.

Suddenly the female interpreter pointed to a building not far from the center of the explosion. "My family is in that house!" If any of the terp's family was still alive, they were facing imminent catastrophe. Five more tractor trailers loaded with Scud missiles and ammunition were parked along the street. Hanks and Sojda looked at each other. "We need to do something, there's people in there," said Hanks.

BOOM. More artillery rounds detonated. Fully aware of the danger, Hanks, Sojda, Bryan, and two other Marines took off for the house. They were running for their lives, braving the mortar blasts in a race against the clock to save any survivors in the building before another tractor trailer went up. *This is it. It's pretty much up the gut or get killed,*" Sojda was thinking. They found nobody alive in the building, and ran back through the danger zone to the tracks. Then the interpreter spoke again.

"No, no. That house." The interpreter pointed to another house across the street from the first.

Back into the danger zone. This time, the Marines made a bee-line through the large crater created by the initial explosion. Hanks and Sojda moved side-by-side, with Bryan and the others trailing behind them.

Hanks led the Marines into the house. A plump Iraqi tottered out of the wreckage. His eyelids were gone, his left eye was hanging out, and his shin bone was exposed by a huge gash. "Got him," said one of the Marines, who put an arm under the wounded man's shoulder and helped him start walking toward the safety of the tracks. On their way back, they were bowled over by the concussion of an exploding mortar shell. Adrenaline flooded through the fat man's body, enabling him to get up and run.

Screams from other people trapped inside the building filled the air. "You guys go next door," barked Sojda. Lance Corporal Bryan went to the next house and led several badly shaken Iraqi teenagers to the safety of the tracks.

More civilians, blackened from the explosion, stumbled out of nearby apartments. The Marines helped the wounded Iraqis back to the tracks even as mortar rounds continued to detonate. The last person to emerge from the building was Michael Hanks, carrying a bleeding five-year-old girl. Hanks ran past the burning arty rounds and delivered the girl into the arms of the corpsman in the tracks.

Once the survivors had been moved to safety, Hanks, with his cocky grin, said, "If I'd known it would be that much trouble, I'd have let the dirty hajjis die." It was a joke, of course. Michael Hanks was a protector, "always had the backs of those around him." It was a principle that Sojda and Hanks would preach incessantly—and put into practice—as they trained the "new" 1st Platoon back at Camp Pendleton.

"We Were One"

1

Boots

Privates, lance corporals, and sergeants are the tip of the spear.

—*Author*

MARCH 2004, CAMP PENDLETON, CALIFORNIA: The "boots" finally arrived. The sun had already set when over two dozen newly minted Marines jumped off the massive seven-ton truck that had carried them up a winding mountain road to a bombed-out village. The Marines were mostly eighteen and nineteen years old, earned about thirteen thousand dollars, and hailed from all parts of the country. The Leathernecks had recently graduated from the School of Infantry (SOI), where Marines fresh from boot camp learn weapons handling and basic combat tactics, and emerge as infantrymen or "grunts." According to one veteran Marine, "the whole platoon was nothing but boots, guys fresh out of SOI. These guys didn't know nothing, not a damn thing. You can't describe how green is green."

As the men climbed off the truck they were greeted sternly by sandy-haired, blue-eyed, twenty-two-year-old Bill Sojda. "I'm Lance Corporal Sojda, your squad leader for 3rd Squad, 1st Platoon. Do you need anything? Chow?"

"No, lance corporal," the new Marines responded in unison.

"Alright, get your sleeping bags, and dress warm; it gets cold around here at night. No smoking. Reveille is at 0430 sharp."

After the brief introduction, Sojda and his pal from his own SOI days—the burly, outgoing Lance Corporal Michael Hanks—let the boots turn in. In an act of striking kindness, the senior men took turns at "firewatch," guarding 3rd Squad's temporary bivouac area while the new men slept. In the Marine Corps, boots are usually relegated to the unsavory duties, like posting firewatch, immediately upon arrival from basic training.

Nearly a year had passed since the daring rescue in Sadr City. Upon Lima Company's return from Iraq, 1st Platoon had been turned into a shell of its former self. Most of the platoon's sergeants shipped off to other units or out of the Corps. A Marine platoon at full strength numbers about forty-six, but for several months 1st Platoon had only a handful of men. Despite its diminutive size, the platoon continued to train, though the men also enjoyed long stretches of hanging out at the barracks, playing PlayStation and waiting for the "boot drop." Sojda and Hanks were relieved when the platoon finally started to fill out.

First Platoon was broken down into three rifle squads. Each of these consisted of about thirteen Marines,* led by a sergeant or by

---

*Typical Marine Corps unit organization and strength are as follows:

Division	15,000+
Regiment	5,000+
Battalion	1,000+
Company	185+
Platoon	46+
Squad	13
Fire team	4

The number of personnel is subject to change based on the unit's mission.

the ranking Marine. Each squad was further divided into three fire teams. First Platoon was one of four platoons comprising Lima Company. Lima, India, and Kilo Companies were the three line companies in the Third Battalion, First Marine Regiment (3/1). Along with headquarters staff, administrative and supply troops, and attached combat specialists, 3rd Battalion had a complement of about one thousand Marines.

The core of each platoon was its most experienced Marines. In 1st Platoon, the core consisted of three lance corporals, all in 3rd Squad. The acting 3rd Squad leader was Bill Sojda, who was joined by Hanks and fellow Sadr City vet Mario Alavez.

The temperature had dipped below 40 degrees and the stars were at their brightest when the boots' rest was interrupted by Hanks's stentorian voice: "Get your asses up." At exactly 0430 the men emerged from their sleeping bags and got their bearings. Their bivouac area, nestled in the hills of Camp Pendleton, California, is known as "Old MOUT Town." MOUT is the acronym for Military Operations in Urban Terrain, the most dangerous form of infantry combat. Featuring several rundown buildings and a burned-out, Vietnam-era AAV, Old MOUT Town is used to teach Marines how to fight in city streets and buildings. After splashing water on their faces, the men folded their sleeping bags, straightened out their uniforms, and filed into formation.

"I don't care where all of you come from, if you were in a gang or whatever. You are going to do what I tell you to do and how I tell you to do it," barked Sojda. "We are going back to Iraq whether you like it or not. We have certain ways of doing things around here and that's how they're going to be done, period. In combat, there's no time for what-ifs. You can what-if yourself to death. If you have time to think in combat, you are probably going to die. You have to make quick decisions."

Then Hanks introduced himself. "I'm Lance Corporal Hanks, 1st Team Leader. I've been through two combat deployments. First at Failaka Island, Kuwait, where fucking terrorists gunned down Corporal Tony Sledd of this platoon in cold blood; later in OIF (Operation Iraqi Freedom), when we made the drive to Baghdad and we were shot at practically the entire time. If you guys think you know everything, you don't. If you are really looking forward to combat, you are going to change your mind as soon as you get there, and you aren't going to want to be there."

Next, Sojda started the process of forging the platoon into a fighting unit, by "first building trust, then creating a family, followed up by training." Sojda began by asking everyone to introduce themselves and tell the group their background, stories about their families, and something embarrassing. "It's a little weird at first, but the more you know about somebody, the better you work with them," Sojda explained. "Hanks and I knew everything about each other, we were best friends, we got to know each other's deepest darkest secrets."

The first to speak was Sojda. The tough-as-nails Marine joined the Corps eight months after graduating from high school. He was motivated in part by patriotism, but also to follow in the footsteps of his father, who had served with the Marines in the battle of Hue City, Vietnam. The former high school football player hoped to use the training he received in the Corps to become a state trooper.

Mike Hanks told the group he wanted to be a Marine most of his life. He tried to join the Corps when he was seventeen, but his mother made him wait until he turned eighteen before allowing him to make the momentous decision. Hanks reported to the Marine recruiter's office on his eighteenth birthday. Because he scored extremely high marks on his entrance exams, the recruiters wanted to know if he would like to go into intelligence or some other specialized field, but Hanks insisted he wanted infantry: "I want to take hills and shoot people."

Nineteen-year-old Nick Larson of Wheaton, Illinois, joined the Marines as a stepping stone to becoming a Navy SEAL. His bedroom wall contained the names of every Navy SEAL killed in action from the Vietnam War through Afghanistan and Iraq—and he had memorized each one of their stories. Shortly after graduating from high school, the avid body builder took a train to the SEAL base on Coronado Island in San Diego and impressed the base commander with his determination and physical prowess.

Larson's "something embarrassing" anecdote sent his comrades into stitches. Known for his rugged good looks, Larson "always had a lot of girls," until he got engaged to his girlfriend, a model. The platoon rolled with laughter when Larson asked rhetorically, "Is it normal for a woman to have a seven-inch clit?" Apparently, a high school friend of Larson's had gone to bed with a woman who turned out to be a pre-operative transsexual.

Larson was inseparable from his best friend from SOI, Private First Class Jacob de la Garza. Garza, a soft-spoken, olive-skinned Latino from Edinburg, Texas, was twenty-one years old and married. "Ever since I was small I wanted to be a Marine," he told the assembled platoon. For many of the men, becoming a Marine was akin to being called into a religious order such as the Jesuits.

Nineteen-year-old Private First Class Nathan Wood of Kirkland, Washington, said he joined the Corps in order to become a man. A lover of fishing, hiking, and camping, Wood considered a career in the Forest Service, but he was drawn into the Corps by its tradition of toughness. Like many of the men, his parents begged him not to join the Marines. After completing his tour of duty, he dreamed of opening a bar called "Stick."

A number of the men were attracted by the structure and the opportunity to make a fresh start offered by the Marine Corps. Wood's good buddy from SOI, Private First Class Steven Wade of Texarkana, Arkansas, left college to make a new beginning in the Marine Corps. Even at the tender age of twenty, Wade was one of the older 0311s, the Marine designation for riflemen. Wade, who looked like a youthful version of Morgan Freeman, called Wood "the white me, the white Wade."

Twenty-three-year-old Mario Alavez had joined the Corps two years earlier to get himself off the mean streets of Houston, Texas. A happily married first-generation Mexican-American, Alavez said, "I wasn't doing the right things with my life," so he dropped out of community college and signed up for the Marines. "I knew the Corps had some hard core shit, so I wanted to see what I was made of, see if I could do it."

Alavez's buddy, twenty-one-year-old Lance Corporal Dustin Turpen, was one of the more experienced Marines. Turpen joined the Corps after seeing the Twin Towers fall on September 11, 2001. In addition to his patriotic motivation, Turpen felt a need to "straighten out my life." Turpen was also inspired by his grandfather, a Marine who fought on Okinawa during World War II. "I was the only person he ever talked to about the war. At Okinawa he lost all of his friends, including his best friend, who died in his arms."

Sojda expected each Marine to buddy up with another Marine. Buddies would do everything together—if one man had to go to the restroom, the other stood outside. The buddy system guaranteed that nobody was ever alone on the battlefield. For most of the men it was a natural extension of the deep friendships they forged at SOI. Accordingly, Sojda had already been buddied up with Hanks for two years. Garza and Larson were so inseparable they were called "Garson," and Wood and Wade were always together. The other men followed suit, finding buddies and establishing partnerships that, for many Marines, become lifelong friendships.

Over the next few days, Sojda and Hanks conducted a crash course in everything from weapons handling to urban combat. "I was given a huge stack of books and manuals, practically three-feet high," recalled one of the boots, Lance Corporal Derick Lowe. Lowe, a former 275-pound, all-state middle linebacker, who was expected to be a starter for the University of Washington, gave up his football career and joined the Marines to put food on the table for his new wife and child. He shed seventy pounds to be accepted by the Marines. "Read up on it, know it, because we are getting into it."

The young Marines were expected to plow through the voluminous tomes and to know their stuff, quickly. Sojda placed special emphasis on medevac training, drilling the men endlessly on getting wounded Marines out of harm's way. Hanks was the enforcer. "If a guy didn't know the proper procedure, we took him behind the bush and hazed him." Mario Alavez put it more bluntly: "When someone puts a boot in your ass, I don't care who you are, eventually you will learn."

Hanks may have been the tough guy, but the men loved him. According to Garza, "There was always a point to the things he taught us. He liked to have fun; no matter what happened, he had a smile on his face. He was always making something into a joke. He made it a lot easier for us, he always protected us like an older brother. Whenever we needed something, he got on the ball and got it for us. One time I needed something for my wife and he got it for me. I couldn't pay my car payment, they needed it by credit card; he made it happen, stuff like that."

The training was intense and fast paced, with Sojda and Hanks promoting a sense of urgency. There was so much to learn in very little time: the platoon was headed for Iraq in less than four months.

The main focus of the training at Old MOUT Town was urban fighting. Firing blanks and "sims," or rounds fitted with a paintball projectile, the platoon used the beat-up concrete blockhouses to learn the proper techniques for clearing enemies out of buildings.

Clearing is more an art than a science, but normally a ten- or eleven-man squad or fire team "stacks"—or lines up—on the side of the house. Each Marine in the stack has a sector to cover: high, low, rear, and the most dangerous area, the "fatal front" or "fatal funnel of fire," where most of a room's defenders aim their fire. The crucial players piercing the fatal front are known as the Number One man and Number Two man. They create a "breach," typically through a door, either by kicking it open or blowing it open with explosives. Before entering a room, the Marines usually slam in a hand grenade, to stun, disorient, or—ideally—kill any enemy combatants occupying the room. Next, the Number One man charges through the entrance, followed by the Number Two man. As they enter the room, they spray their weapons into the fatal funnel, and then hit the corners. Then they sweep back and scan the rest of the room, pointing out danger areas, booby traps, hallways, doors, and other hiding places. The team sounds off "clear" if the room is free of the enemy and moves to the next room. As the Number One and Number Two men clear additional rooms in the building, other members of the squad team provide security in the rooms just cleared, so the enemy cannot reoccupy. The key is momentum and keeping the enemy off balance.

In the real world, things rarely work out like the textbooks. According to one senior Marine NCO, "The training is just a baseline. There are a thousand variations to clearing a room. There are so many things that can throw you off, such as what if a couch catches on fire from a grenade or the room is filled with dust and debris after the grenade went off and you can't see in the room (a common occurrence in the stone houses in Iraq). Plus, you didn't want to set a pattern so the enemy could anticipate how we clear rooms. We would adjust to keep them guessing. We taught our guys to improvise and modify things based on the variables they encountered."

Sojda and Hanks rode the men hard at Old MOUT Town, training from dawn until late in the evening. But once they got back to Camp Pendleton and turned in their weapons, 1st Platoon lost its momentum. Lima's company commander had just become a father, and he allowed his newborn child to distract him from training his Marines. According to one of Lima Company's NCOs, the captain practiced "leadership through intimidation," while providing "minimal guidance." The captain even allegedly discouraged the men from training on their own. "Every time we'd try stuff we'd get our ass chewed," recalled Sojda. Other Marines were more sanguine, and considered the Marine captain "a nice guy who was just preoccupied."

Nevertheless, as the acting squad leaders, Sojda and Hanks took it upon themselves to train the fledgling platoon. "We knew we had to do something. In three months we were going to Iraq, so we did anything we could around the barracks, dug fighting holes, built sand tables, and even practiced changing magazines and house clearing with brooms," recalled Sojda.

The training regimen got back on track with the arrival of thirty-year-old Staff Sergeant Matthew Hackett, who was promoted to gunnery sergeant in November 2004. Born and raised in Seattle, Washington, Hackett finished high school early, did a semester in college, and joined the Corps at age seventeen. Married for ten years, and the father of one child, the experienced NCO was known for staying cool and making quick, correct decisions under the most trying circumstances. He was also passionate about making 1st Platoon the best platoon in Lima Company. Hackett took over the leadership role Sojda had been filling, and built on the efforts of Sojda and Hanks. "I trained the trainers, the people who will train the new guys. Essentially I told guys like Hanks and Sojda what we have and where we want to go. Let's give them the tools so they can take the ball and run with it for the new guys. Guys like Sojda trained the others on tactics. The men saw that their sergeants really cared about them. They might get a hard time for not learning something, but they knew 'these guys really care about me. They will do anything to ensure that I survive and make it through this.'"

As 1st Platoon filled up with Marines, each of the three squads assumed its own persona, largely reflecting the temperaments of their leaders. Hanks and Sojda's 3rd Squad, the heart of the platoon, was described as "too cool for school" or the "rough riders." Second and 1st Squads seemed more stoic.

Lacking a sergeant, 2nd Squad's senior NCO was Corporal Adel Abudayeh, known simply as Abu. Abu had been with Lima Company during Operation Iraqi Freedom (OIF). As an experienced MOUT trainer, he was a great asset to the green platoon. Dark-skinned and with salt-and-pepper hair, Abudayeh was of Middle Eastern and Latin descent.

One of 2nd Squad's fire teams was led by twenty-one-year-old Corporal Kevin Myirski, a champion weight lifter from Camden, Pennsylvania. Myirski joined the Corps right out of high school in order to "start a real life, real fast."

Lance Corporal Heath Kramer, another 2nd Squad fire team leader, was a muscular, five-foot seven-inch standout wrestler from Mantua, Ohio. Kramer had the mental toughness only wrestling breeds. After enduring years of grueling practices, Kramer trained his men hard, because he wanted the Marines in his fire team to be ready before they got into combat.

One of 2nd Squad's most colorful characters was Lance Corporal Craig James III, a short, stocky, twenty-year-old African-American from inner-city Chicago. The sharp-witted James was an expert dice thrower and easily one of the funniest men in the platoon, James modeled his sense of humor after comedian Bernie Mack. James was joined by Private Marshall Kennedy, a tall, bespectacled youth from rural Arkansas with a thick southern drawl. When asked where he was from, he'd reply, "Arsaw." Kennedy, known for his patriotism and deep loyalty to his friends, was also following in the footsteps of relatives who'd served in the Corps. Nicknamed "Butters," from the popular cartoon series *South Park*, Kennedy didn't quite hit it off initially with his team leader, Kramer. Many of the men fondly remember Kramer hammering Butters for an infraction: "I'll climb you like a tree and beat you like a stump." It was no idle threat. Wrestlers of Kramer's caliber never lose a grappling contest. Later, despite their differences in rank, the two men became close friends.

The lowest-ranking member of 2nd Squad was twenty-one-year-old Private Sean Stokes, of Sacramento, California. Ironically, Stokes, who bore a resemblance to Luke Skywalker of *Star Wars*, was one of the most senior riflemen in the platoon. After serving for a year, Stokes was court-martialed for leaving the base without permission, even though his motive was pure: he was helping a relative escape from domestic violence. Having been busted to the lowest rank in the Corps, Stokes was offered a second chance with Lima Company. "My old unit did not see combat, I had no respect for them. I was told 3/1 was going to Iraq to go kill the enemy. I said I was here to kill the enemy. It was the change of pace I was looking for. 3/1 gave me another shot."

Stokes would prove to be invaluable to the platoon in Iraq. Stokes's best friend was Lance Corporal Benjamin Bryan, a fire team leader in 1st Squad. Bryan, from Lumberton, North Carolina, fondly known as the "Opossum." Bryan took life day by day, usually kept to himself, and seldom got upset about anything. Known for his prowess at video games, Bryan's ambition after the Corps was to drive a Budweiser truck.

To those who did not know him, Bryan's laid back attitude could leave the impression that he did not care about his fellow Marines, but nothing was further from the truth. A few months after the remnants of 1st Platoon returned from Sadr City in 2003, they conducted cold weather training at Bridgeport, located in the mountains of northern California. The men were on a "death march" through Bridgeport's snow-packed mountains when one Marine went into convulsions and hypothermia. Bryan took the Marine's pack off, gently put the man on the ground, and combined both their sleeping bags. Next he took off his clothes and used his body heat to revive the Marine. His body warmth stabilized the dying Marine long enough for a medevac to arrive and save the man's life.

Several members of 1st Squad also had criminal records. One Marine was told bluntly by a judge, "You have a choice, jail time or the Corps." Serving in the Marine Corps could turn a man's life around. The Corps offers any man a chance for redemption.

2

A Grunt's Grunt

Regard your soldiers as your children, and they will follow you into the deepest valleys; look on them as your own beloved sons, and they will stand by you even unto death.

— *Sun Tzu*, The Art of War

FIRST PLATOON EXPERIENCED A WATERSHED EVENT ON April 5, 2004: the arrival of 3rd Squad's leader, Sergeant James "Bennie" Conner. The twenty-eight-year-old feisty Irishman was a five-foot, three-inch ball of energy. Known as the "Leprechaun" or "Seamus," the dark and handsome Conner looked like a Marine sergeant from the Hollywood set of *The Sands of Iwo Jima*—a good week into the battle. Conner's signature stubble and unbloused trouser legs skirted the regulations calling for Marines to be clean shaven, even in combat, with pants tucked tidily into their boots. "I'm kind of dirty. Half the time I don't wash my face. I have my sleeves halfway rolled up. I'm kind of tiny, so if I have my sleeves all the way down, they get wrapped around my thumbs. By unblousing my trousers, it lets my feet and legs breathe. I don't do it to spite anyone, it's my idea of what a grunt is all about, a dirty person. The guys in the Spec Ops community are also unconventional; they have a look, they're cool. The bottom line is that I get the job done, and it works for me."

Born and raised in Delaware, Conner wanted to be a Marine his entire life. During his seven years in the Corps, Conner had already served several tours of duty overseas, including combat in Operation Iraqi Freedom. He was itching to return to battle and the comradeship that comes with leading a squad of Marines.

However, to return to combat, Conner needed the Marine Corps to give him a second chance. Months earlier, he had been busted while off duty for public urination at a Taco Bell after a night of drinking. It was a one-time slip up, but the incident relegated Conner to a stateside support unit, destined to sit out the war in Iraq.

Opportunity knocked when Conner spotted 3/1's pragmatic and charismatic commanding officer, Lieutenant Colonel Willard Buhl, working out in one of Camp Pendleton's many weight rooms. Possessing a secondary military occupational specialty in military intelligence, Buhl was well-suited to lead 3/1. The diminutive sergeant screwed up his courage and approached the senior officer. "Excuse me, sir, are you the battalion CO for 3/1?" Buhl nodded and said, "Yeah, what's up, devil dog?" With a hearty laugh, Conner said, "I need a job."

After hearing the story, Buhl sent Conner to speak with the battalion Sergeant Major Edward Sax, who had served with Conner in another unit. The sergeant major looked Conner squarely in the face and said, "You don't need to deploy, you've already been on three deployments. We are going to Iraq."

Conner responded, "I kind of messed up. I only want a chance to redeem myself."

"Are you sure? This is going to be a tough one."

"I'm positive."

The sergeant major offered his hand. "Okay, you belong to me, go check in with Lima Company."

The next day, Staff Sergeant Hackett assigned Conner to 3rd Squad. Conner joined his new men in the bus on their way to the firing range. Conner didn't speak to anybody during the trip, and the men were puzzled about him. Derick Lowe remembers his first impression of the Leprechaun: "Pant legs undone, scruffy, five-o'clock shadow." Like the rest of them, Lowe was thinking, *"Who the hell is this guy?"*

Sojda was the first to find out. Once they arrived at the firing range, Conner approached him directly and said, "I've heard good things about you. I don't want to take your job as squad leader, but I'm a sergeant."

For Sojda it was a hard blow, especially after he'd been leading the squad for months, but he calmly said to Conner, "I know. It's cool, Sergeant."

Conner gave a brief pep talk to his new Marines. "I've been in the infantry for six-and-a-half years, I know my business. Not to insult anyone. I don't know you and you don't know me. But we are going to start from the beginning and practice."

Under Conner, 3rd Squad continued practicing the basic things that mean life or death in battle. From changing an M16 magazine to proper room clearing techniques. From the difference between cover and concealment to basic radio operating skills. But Conner placed even greater emphasis on reaching the men's minds.

When the squad took a break from the basics he would give the men a "moto" speech. "Moto" is Marinespeak for motivation and dedication to Corps and mission. Conner held fast to the Marine traditions of duty, honor, and loyalty. He reminded the men again and again that the Corps is the greatest fighting force in the world, a point most Marines will make to anyone who will listen. On the personal level, Conner stressed adaptability and boldness.

Conner's moto talks often emphasized strengthening the relationships within the squad. Conner frequently asked the men about their families, girlfriends, wives, and why they joined. "I'd talk to my guys and make them feel comfortable, build that bond. I'll be there when you need me; I rarely yelled at anyone. I'd rather work with somebody," recalled Conner.

"Conner made us get close to one another and tried to understand how everyone thought, so when we went into combat, we knew what everyone was thinking," remembered Derick Lowe.

Overcoming fear was another important aspect of Conner's training. He trained his men to stay alive and not fear combat. "It's war, people are going to die in war, but there's things you can do to not be one of the dead. You should not fear dying; once you are dead, you don't feel it." Ultimately, building relationships and friendships within the squad made the men rely on each other, and, if necessary, die for one other. This type of unit cohesion is the nucleus of the Marine Corps ethos and is the fundamental principle upon which all Marines are indoctrinated from day one in basic training. "The Corps is you and you are the Corps." Another Marine's blood being spilled is your own blood, a part of you. It is this way of thinking that keeps men from regressing to childhood in combat. Devoid of any sense of individuality or selfishness, that paradigm, a mindset of strength and solidarity, keeps them from crawling inside of themselves in horror when bullets start flying.

Marines usually address each other using rank and last name, but Conner wanted to form the squad into a family, so he dropped the titles. "Most of the Corps doesn't usually call each other by first names, but as you can see, my guys did. They called me Bennie, or Leprechaun, or Seamus. If I'm mortally wounded and lying there with my guts hanging out, I don't want somebody coming up to me saying, 'Hey Sergeant Conner, you're going to be all right.' You better call me by my name, since it might be the last time I hear it."

On the day of Conner's arrival, Hanks was in court facing a DUI (driving under the influence) charge. While Hanks may not have been present physically, he was still, as usual, the focus of attention in 1st Platoon. Conner repeatedly heard the men telling stories about "this guy Hanks, Hanks this, Hanks that." The men in the Corps like to draw a distinction between "field" Marines and "garrison" Marines. Hanks was not much of a spit and polish garrison Marine. He was infamous for his off-base antics, often revolving around a few cold beers, but he had already proven his worthiness on the battlefield.

The following day, Conner noticed a "real slob" hanging around his platoon.

"Who the fuck are you, man?" snapped Conner.

"I'm Lance Corporal Hanks."

"Didn't you just get out of traffic court?"

Conner quickly recognized a kindred spirit. "I liked Hanks immediately. My parents would always tell me, 'I hope someday you have a kid just like you.' I was a hellraiser as a young kid, and always in trouble. I got one in Hanks." The two men bonded right away.

Conner needed to build 3rd Squad around the leaders of his three four-man fire teams. Sojda was the leader of the first team. If the Leprechaun was hit, Sojda would assume command of 3rd Squad. Conner quickly chose Hanks to lead the second fire team. Several days later, Conner went over his team leader selections with Staff Sergeant Hackett. "Sojda, and Ha— . . ."

Conner was cut off in midsentence.

"Naaah. It's never going to fly," said Hackett.

"I want Hanks as my second team leader," insisted Conner.

"First sergeant is never going to approve it."

"That's what I want. Can you at least run it by him?"

"If it doesn't work, pick someone else," said Hackett. "I'll run it by him. But if he gets in trouble, it's your ass."

"That's fine with me," Conner fired back confidently.

Hanks was eventually approved, and with the fire team leaders chosen, 3rd Squad was finally taking shape.

Shortly after Conner joined the platoon, 2nd and 1st Squads also received their squad leader sergeants. Sergeant Jason Kyle, a twenty-six-year-old from Chagrin Falls, Ohio, took over 2nd Squad. Married with a child, Kyle had six years in the Corps, and had even completed a tour of duty guarding the U.S. Embassy in Moscow. The seasoned African-American NCO, known for his cool, competent leadership style, instantly won the respect of the men in his squad.

Sergeant Juan Calderon, who would command 1st Squad, was the last to arrive. As a former Marine assaultman, a specialist in weapons and explosives, Calderon was well versed in tactics and equipment. He also liked to teach himself languages, including Arabic. The ultracompetitive Marine loved to talk trash on the basketball court, claiming he could whip anybody one-on-one. According to all accounts, he never lost a game. The brown-eyed, black-haired Texan was married to the "love of his life," who was pregnant with their first child.

Most of the platoon was in place when the new platoon commander arrived in mid-April. Six-foot-tall, blond-haired, blue-eyed Second Lieutenant Jeffrey Sommers was twenty-two years old. With his ramrod-straight posture and good looks, Sommers had the presence of a movie star. Sommers's looks led some members of the platoon to think he was a "pretty boy." However, the new second lieutenant was a born leader, whose leadership style was similar to World War II hero and platoon leader Dick Winters, of *Band of Brothers* fame.

The Naval Academy graduate came from a military family. Sommers grew up near West Point, and the armed forces had always appealed to him. Sommers said he liked "the idea of being part of something greater than yourself, plus there's traveling, and always doing something interesting and being in front of world politics." At Annapolis, Sommers studied mechanical engineering, but the greatest lesson he learned was that loyalty is the most important element of any military unit. "Shared misery or shared adversity bonds men together."

Training accelerated at breakneck speed. Over the next six weeks, 1st Platoon would participate in three major training exercises.

Third Battalion's first large field operation was held during April 2004, at one of the most advanced tactical-level live-fire training facilities in the world, the Marine Corps Air–Ground Combat Center in Twentynine Palms, California. Nestled in the Mojave Desert's Chocolate Mountains, Twentynine Palms is a few hours from Camp Pendleton. The Combat Center conducts the Combined Arms Exercise (CAX) program, which uses live ammunition to approximate actual battlefield conditions. The Thundering Third would be part of a team of ground troops, armor, artillery, and aircraft that would engage and destroy a fictitious enemy.

During the exercise, the battalion maneuvered, both on foot and mounted in vehicles, through live-ordnance impact areas, as helicopters and fixed-wing aircraft dropped real bombs. The platoon practiced attacking fortified positions, operating convoys, breaching obstacles, and coordinating air strikes. The war games take into account equipment breakdowns and other constraints found in combat. CAX is meant to get as close to combat as possible without actually being there.

The exercise was also designed specifically to prepare 3/1 for the upcoming assault on Fallujah. Located west of Baghdad, the city had become the main hub of the mujahideen, the Islamist opponents of the U.S.-led coalition's occupation of Iraq.

In March 2004, four American contractors had been murdered, mutilated, and hung from a bridge in front of screaming Fallujah crowds. Over the next month, the city swelled with foreign and al-Qaeda fighters. The city could not be subdued by political means; Fallujah would have to be taken on the ground. The Thundering Third, along with the bulk of the 1st Marine Regiment, was headed to Fallujah to do the job.

The battalion's next major "training evolution" was a Security and Stabilization Operations (SASO) field exercise at the former George Air Force Base in Victorville, California, from April 24 through 28. The base's abandoned buildings frequently served as mock villages for honing MOUT skills, but the primary purpose of this exercise was to prepare the men for dealing with the civilian population in Iraq. In a sense, the Marines in Iraq faced a greater challenge than their predecessors in World War II. They had to function as peacekeepers and police officers, not just as assault forces. The SASO exercise taught them how to interact with both hostile and friendly civilian populations. According to Conner, SASO was "common sense" training. "They taught you how to turn it on and turn it off, when to be aggressive and when not to be aggressive." Hanks snidely derided SASO as "sunshine and lollipops" because it was not offensive in nature.

Seventy Marines from the 1st Battalion, 1st Marines, served as the OPFOR, or opposing force. The OPFOR dressed in civilian clothes to simulate Iraqi and al-Qaeda terrorist cells. During one patrol, the OPFOR caught 1st Platoon with simulated IEDs (improvised explosive devices), the roadside bombs responsible for at least a third of American deaths in Iraq. In general, however, the men stayed one step ahead of the OPFOR. According to 1st Platoon's radio operator, twenty-year-old Colorado native Lance Corporal Bradley Adams, "We patrolled constantly and paid attention to everything."

The OPFOR also tried to overrun 1st Platoon's "firm base," the house where they holed up for the night. "They were sloppy and tried to rush the wire. We had two or three SAWs (squad automatic weapons) lightin' up," recalled Stokes.

During the SASO training exercise, the platoon started coming together as a team. Sojda's obsession with casualty evacuation paid off, as 1st Platoon aced the mock CASEVAC exercises, leaving no fallen Marines behind.

On April 29, the battalion hosted the "Bloody George–3/1 Guidon Adoption Ceremony." History plays a central role in Marine training. Stories about the great battles are told and retold by the Marines of the present day, who extol the achievements of Marines past with a religious passion. Battles like Belleau Wood, Iwo Jima, the Chosin Reservoir, and Hue City are like Scripture to the Marine Corps. Lieutenant Colonel Buhl was particularly knowledgeable about the history of his battalion. Whenever possible, he invited Marines from the past wars to address his men.

As the battalion prepared to go into battle once more, Buhl invited all 3/1 combat veterans to attend the ceremony in honor of George Company, 3rd Battalion, 1st Marines, who earned great glory during the Korean War. Many distinguished veterans from World War II, Korea, and Vietnam attended. According to 3/1's Command Chronology, the purpose of the ceremony was to commemorate "G/3/1's superior service in the face of intense, prolonged combat operations in Korea." During the massive Chinese surprise attack that drove UN forces out of the northern half of Korea, fighting bitter cold as well as a determined enemy, George Company held a key hill at the southern tip of the Chosin Reservoir for several days against thousands of Chinese soldiers. George Company's heroic resistance allowed thousands of Marines to escape annihilation at the "Frozen Chosin." The highlight of the ceremony was the rededication of the George Company guidon. George Company's flag "shall be carried into combat yet again, for service in Operation Iraqi Freedom II."

After a couple of weeks of downtime and equipment maintenance, Lima Company went on another training exercise, beginning on May 10 at March Air Force Base. The exercise included more of Hanks's "sunshine and lollipop" drills, and also emphasized MOUT training, since 3/1 would be clearing houses in Fallujah. The intensity of the training was ratcheted up. "Lima Company was put through a ballbreaking pace and the platoon was trained on how to search a house, how to capture high-value targets. They were also constantly hit with IEDs, sniper attacks, RPGs, and complex ambushes," recalled a Marine instructor from March AFB.

This exercise included the use of tanks for a battalion-sized unit. During the exercise, 3/1's commander, Lieutenant Colonel Buhl, placed special emphasis on teaching his "ground-pounders" how to work with tanks. Close coordination between infantry and armor had become an essential aspect of American military doctrine for urban combat. Buhl also knew 3/1 was going to lead the assault on Fallujah. Tank training was crucial.

Complementing the training, Conner continued his efforts to turn his squad into a family. When the sun went down and the men "went firm," or bivouacked for the evening, the squad would relax together and tell stories about girls, parties, bars, and OIF I. Hanks, the master storyteller and comedian, usually led the conversation. According to Conner, "We really started to get tight."

After completing the third training exercise, the Lima Company went to the beach. Bonfires lit up the sky as actor and former Marine Gunnery Sergeant Lee Ermey addressed the men. Ermey, host of the popular History Channel show *Mail Call*, is famous for his archetypal portrayal of a drill instructor in the movie *Full Metal Jacket*.

The gunny went through his entire drill instructor routine from the opening act of Stanley Kubrick's famous movie, which ironically culminates with the Fallujah of Vietnam, the battle of Hue City. "I'm Gunnery Sergeant Hartman, your senior drill instructor. From now on, you will speak only when spoken to. The first word out of your filthy sewers will be 'Sir.' Do you maggots understand? . . ."

The entire battalion was on their knees with laughter. The Marines were "loving it, and everyone was getting really trashed," recalled Sommers.

Throughout the evening, Kramer had been pestering Kennedy, the lanky teenager from Arkansas, to "stand up and say something." The wobbly youth finally arose, and with a slight slur, said, "My team leader wanted me to get up. All I have to say is I love this company."

First Platoon responded in unison, "Butters, shut the fuck up."

"I want some of what you are drinking," said Ermey, giving the audience a hearty chuckle.

The beach party passed as quickly as it began, and the battalion went back to Camp Pendleton to prepare to ship out to Iraq. During the first week in May, the camp saw frenzied activity as weapons were cleaned, equipment inventoried, and Humvees packed up. The men placed their gear out in front of them at the parade ground for inspection by the company commander and battalion commander. The Marines worked around the clock. Everything had to be ready before the men could go on their final leave before departing for Iraq in June.

At 9:00 or 10:00 every night, the exhausted Marines would gather, beer in hand, for a bit of relaxation. Hanks, Sojda, and several others who had fought in Iraq, including sniper Sergeant Greg Smith, told the boots their combat stories, especially the stories about 1st Platoon's experiences in Iraq and Kuwait.

The men described Lima Company's nine-hour firefight during the battle of Nasiriyah and ambushes in Sadr City. The focal point became the coldblooded terrorist assault on Failaka Island in Kuwait, when Corporal Antonio J. Sledd was gunned down by al-Qaeda operatives, and the unarmed platoon, in the midst of a stickball game, received its baptism by fire.

The square-jawed, battle-hardened Smith nearly lost his life at Failaka Island. Raised in Somers, Connecticut, in a family with a strong military tradition, Smith wanted to serve his country from childhood. Smith's grandfather was one of the men in the first wave of the heroes who stormed Omaha Beach; he wears his grandfather's dog tags into battle.

Located about twenty kilometers outside Kuwait City, Failaka Island was used by the Marines in October 2002 as a training area. According to Smith, when the attack came, Lima Company was taking a break at their beachside campsite after a morning of MOUT training.

"They said there was no hostile threat. I didn't think about it since we had never been in combat. I remember clearing the houses and we were all tired. We were doing it for four or five hours.

We got back to the beach and started to play a game of stickball. We were just screwing around."

The Marines were stripped to their shorts, barefooted, playing ball in the burning hot desert sun, when two men pulled up in a white Nissan pickup truck with red pinstripes. The men hopped out of the truck fifty yards away from the Marines, and opened up with automatic weapons.

"At first all we heard were gunshots, we didn't know what was going on," recalled Sojda. "The sand started exploding all around us. Everyone started screaming, 'Get down! Get down! Get behind something!' It was so chaotic, there was so many guys diving behind packs, the only thing we could hide behind was our packs on the beach. None of us had our weapons on us; none of us had any ammunition.

"They started walking towards us, spraying, shooting from the hip. They hit Lance Corporal [posthumously promoted corporal] Antonio Sledd. He went down. Lance Corporal George Simpson was wounded. One of the terrorists walked right up to Sledd, point blank, and started shooting across his body. He put rounds in from his lower right hip to his chest. Ripped him in half."

One of the only men in Lima Company carrying a loaded weapon was Lima Company's first sergeant, who had a 9mm pistol. The first sergeant returned fire with deadly effect. He killed the terrorist standing over Sledd, and then knocked down the second terrorist as he retreated toward the pickup. "Before the other guy died, First Sergeant and a whole bunch of us walked up to him. He was bleeding, lying there, saying something in Arabic over and over, and he died."

At that point, the company started taking fire from a nearby fishing village. Caught on an open beach without arms or ammunition, the only option was to dive into the water. "You know how there's a little crest in the ocean. We tried to take cover behind it, half our bodies were in the water," recalled Smith.

While the company sheltered in the surf, one or two men at a time ran to the camp to grab rifles, helmets, and flak jackets. There was no ammunition: the Marines were in serious trouble. Deliverance arrived just in time, in the form of two helicopters.

"All of a sudden green smoke is thrown out. A Blackhawk came down right behind us. I will never forget that. The sound of that Blackhawk coming meant people were going to come save us. Like a movie, we rushed Sledd to the Blackhawk. He bled out on the helicopter. Next, a CH-47 helicopter came in, and they did a hot drop. They dropped the back ramp and we ran up there and grabbed as many ammo crates as we could. We were lying down shoulder to shoulder, passing crates of ammunition over our heads, down the line, so every Marine had at least ten rounds. We were taking a lot of fire from the town."

Once the ammunition was distributed, the company charged the village, secured the first block, and settled into a lengthy firefight. "We were exchanging fire the whole time, shooting motherfuckers deep in the city taking potshots at us. The terrorists were doing, 'Israeli off-hands,' sticking their guns out a window, not looking but pointing and spraying at us." After eight hours, Lima Company was withdrawn from combat.

"Failaka Island affected us so much," recalled Smith. "We had so much hatred for the terrorists. During OIF I, the company was driven by it. We lost one of our brothers. We all had personal vendettas for the terrorists."

Sledd was a close friend of Hanks, Sojda, and Smith. For 1st Platoon's new generation, his death became a rallying cry. "You motherfuckers will remember how and why Sledd died," shouted Hanks. "We need to take care of business!"

During the last hectic weeks of training, Conner, Hanks, Sojda, and the rest of the platoon watched as the first battle of Fallujah played out on their television screens. "We knew we were headed for a 'hot' deployment, we knew we were headed for Fallujah, so I did everything in our power to prepare my Marines," recalled Conner.

Hanks, Sojda, Kramer, and Bryan went beyond the call of duty on behalf of the green Marines. Knowing the boots were not ready for Fallujah, they both extended their terms in the Marine Corps so they could remain with 1st Platoon. The three were nearing their EAS (end of active service), but decided to put their own lives on the line for another deployment, to protect the lives of their brothers in arms.

Once the platoon's equipment was packed, the Marines went on leave: thirty days for most of the boots, and fifteen days for senior Marines like Sojda and Conner, who took turns staying behind to make sure everything remained ready for the trip to Iraq. Most of the men went home to their families. Lowe and Wood made the long journey to Washington by car. Hanks flew to Michigan, to discover that his parents were frantic with worry.

The last weekend before boarding the plane, most of the Marines drank like fish. Hanks and Sojda spent their last weekend in Cali in a drunken stupor. Garza and Larson took it easy, remaining in the barracks to practice changing magazines and clearing rooms. Each man had to handle the stress in his own way.

On June 16, 2004, 1st Platoon, Lima Company, and the rest of the Thundering Third, about one thousand Marines altogether, departed for Iraq.

3

Into the Cauldron

They shall grow not old, as we that are left grow old;
Age shall not weary them, nor the years condemn.
At the going down of the sun and in the morning
We will remember them.

—*Laurence Binyon*, "For the Fallen"

"WELCOME TO KUWAIT. The temperature outside is a hot and dry 113 degrees," droned the flight attendant as Lima Company's chartered airliner touched down. The Marines had spent the grueling twenty-two-hour flight listening to the same "tired" CD of rock and country music, and speculating about their fate. Most of the men were worried; they were heading to Fallujah, the most dangerous city in Iraq. "I didn't want to get out of the plane, and as soon as we got off the plane, the heat hit you quick," recalled a sweaty Private Stokes.

After a brief layover in Kuwait, Lima Company took a military transport plane to the main Marine airbase in Iraq, known as al-Taqaddum Airbase (TQ). For the final leg of the journey, the men jumped into seven-ton trucks that carried them over the winding Iraqi desert roads to Camp Abu Ghraib, about twenty miles outside of Fallujah. To avoid the possibility of ambush, the trucks stayed off the main highways, following less traveled roads that skirted the city.

To the men, Fallujah had an "evil glow," with scattered lights breaking up the outlines of the darkened buildings and the spiky minarets of nearly one hundred mosques. Suddenly the city went black. The private driving 3rd Squad's truck tried hard to look unconcerned, but in a shaky voice he said the muj were about to attack the convoy. Hanks and Sojda, sitting in the cab, just laughed. Is this guy trying to scare us? You can't talk like that to combat veterans. Hanks and Sojda surmised that electrical power inside the city was intermittent, as it had been during their days in Sadr City, so the sudden darkness was not a sign of a pending attack on the convoy. Hanks acidly told the nervous driver to "shut the fuck up." "What a pussy," thought Sojda.

By the time 3/1 reached Fallujah, the city had become a nest of vipers. Soon after Baghdad was liberated and Saddam driven out of power in April 2003, an unlikely alliance of Saddam loyalists and al-Qaeda holy warriors began to concentrate in the city. They worked steadily to undermine the rule of the Coalition. In April 2004, the Marines were ready to reimpose Coalition control by assaulting the city, but the attack was aborted over Coalition fears of a backlash in the Muslim world. The terrorist network declared victory and organized a ruling council called the Mujahideen Shura. The Shura consisted of gangs of "insurgents" made up of former Republican Guards, Baathists, criminals, and foreign fighters from all over the Muslim world. The leader of al-Qaeda in Iraq, archterrorist Abu Musab al-Zarqawi, soon set up shop in Fallujah. Dominated by Zarqawi, the city became a base of operations to export terrorism across Iraq.

Backed by the Coalition and the provisional Iraqi government, several of Saddam's former generals attempted to broker a peace between the mujahideen and the Coalition. The generals said they would use a group of Iraqi troops known as the Fallujah Brigade to maintain order in the city and contain the insurgency. In fact, the brigade largely worked on behalf of the mujahideen, and did nothing to stop the buildup of jihadists inside the city. Fallujah became the center of the mujahideen effort in Iraq. Politics, particularly the fear of inflicting civilian casualties, allowed the insurgency to fester and grow.

Camp Abu Ghraib is an old Iraqi Army base adjacent to the infamous Abu Ghraib Prison.

The Thundering Third arrived at Abu Ghraib to relieve 1st Battalion, 5th Marines, and assume responsibility for guarding the area around the prison and quelling any potential detainee uprisings. The camp and prison were overflowing with Marines. First Platoon and the rest of Lima Company were billeted in stifling canvas tents with plywood floors. Green aluminum cots filled the tents in tightly packed rows. It was a restless night for most of Lieutenant Sommers's Marines, with the temperature outside staying over 100 degrees all night long.

Reveille was at 0600. Michael Hanks was brushing his teeth, while a couple of sleep-deprived young Marines were playing the card game Uno. Most of the sleepy Marines were just crawling out of their cots when they were greeted by the high-pitched whistle of mortar rounds.

"Is that incoming or outgoing?"

"That's incoming!"

In their skivvies and tee shirts, most of the men made a mad rush for their Kevlar helmets and flak vests, scrambled through the tent flaps, and sprinted to nearby bombproof cement bunkers. The flimsy brown tents were death traps; a direct hit from a mortar round could wound or kill most of the platoon, who were packed into the tents like sardines.

Hanks, however, kept on brushing his teeth, Sojda calmly smoked a cigarette, and Conner put in a dip of Copenhagen in his lip. "Why's everybody freaking?" chuckled Hanks.

"Bring it on," snapped Conner. He was thinking, *Hopefully they'll come over the wall.*" The notion that the mujahideen might try to pull off a massive prison break was not farfetched. In fact, insurgents nearly pulled off a massive prison break in the spring of 2005.

Conner, Hanks, and Sojda seemed to have had their nerves snipped. It was not bravado—the well-worn clichés, "you're either afraid or crazy" and "no atheists in foxholes," did not apply to these Marines. They looked forward to action, facing it rather than fearing it. One Marine boiled it down to a single word: "*balls.*" And they were "cool as cucumbers in the shit," something the Corps seeks in all its leaders.

A few days later, Sommers's Marines transferred from their temporary tents to empty cells inside the prison. The men never guarded prisoners, but patrolled the villages outside the walls of the prison. Ironically, their new home was the very prison that later made headlines. Every cell contained meat hooks or a single light bulb dangling from a thin black wire, relics from the days when the prison was used by Saddam's intelligence service to torture Iraqis. The section where the Marines were billeted was within RPG and sniper range of the city of Abu Ghraib, so the men found out going to the head could be a hazardous adventure. But the prison's chow hall, bombproof concrete walls, and creature comforts more than made up for the dangers. "It had a rack (bed), AC, and power. At that point, I don't think I could ask for anything else," recalled Hackett. Compared to most Marines in 3/1, 1st Platoon had it good.

As June came to a close, 3/1 conducted "left seat and right seat" combat operations with 1/5. In layman's terms, they rode around Fallujah with the outgoing unit, getting the lay of the land. The battalion quickly put its SASO training to work, interacting with the locals, while learning about the latest enemy tactics from 1/5. There was very little fighting.

On June 28, 3/1's line companies occupied their command posts. India Company's headquarters was in the Karmah Schoolhouse, Kilo Company took the Oil for Food Warehouse in Shahabi, and Lima Company remained in Abu Ghraib Prison.

First Platoon's area of operation included the area immediately surrounding the prison walls, several tiny hamlets on the western side of Fallujah such as Khandari, and Nasser Wa Salaam, a medium-sized town about five miles from Abu Ghraib. Nasser Wa Salaam consisted of rows of single-story, tan stone houses, apartment buildings, a few palm groves, and a small lake in the center of town. On its first independent patrol, the platoon trudged through Nasser's dusty streets. In June, the temperature in Iraq sears to over 115 degrees Fahrenheit. The bulky body armor, helmets, and long sleeves pushed the Marines' body temperatures past 130 degrees. Cooking under their body armor, they drank bottle after bottle of water to stay hydrated. As his tired Marines trudged from one end of Nasser to the other, Conner was thinking, "*It is so goddamn hot, this patrol is taking forever. Is this town ever going to end?*"

As the Marines walked up and down the streets, most of Nasser Wa Salaam's residents stayed indoors, wondering who the new guys were. Where were the familiar Marines from 1/5? The typical Iraqi village is highly communal, and everybody knows everybody's business. First Platoon, recognizing that establishing relationships with

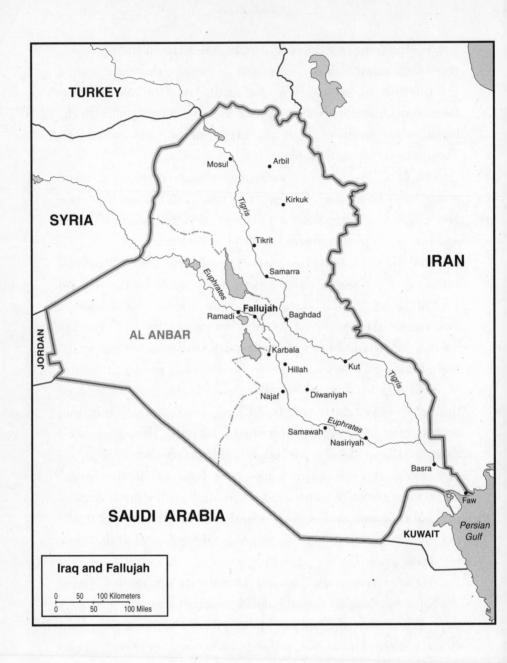

Iraq and Fallujah

0   50   100 Kilometers
0   50   100 Miles

the Iraqis was a key aspect of their job, made a point of introducing themselves to the locals.

The platoon soon learned that making friends with the Iraqis was often a difficult process. The local population wanted security, and generally hated the mujahideen, but befriending Coalition troops could be very risky.

One of the biggest problems in the war effort was that Coalition troops did not live with the villagers. American and Iraqi troops were usually quartered in huge bases. They rolled out of the front gates in their armored Humvees, like a scene from the movie *Mad Max*; patrolled for twelve hours; and retreated behind the fortified walls and wire of their base camp, leaving the villages to the mercy of the mujahideen. The muj targeted people who talked to the Americans. This intimidation campaign, a classical application of Lenin's doctrine of controlling civilian populations by "terrorizing" them, was one of the muj's most effective weapons.

A few weeks later, 1st Platoon, reaching out to "hearts and minds," delivered approximately 1,500 gallons of water to the locals in Nasser Wa Salaam. "Everyone loved us. We didn't have to worry about security. They came up, we gave them water, and helped deliver it to their houses. It was gratifying that we were doing the right thing. These people want us here. Several people came up to us and thanked us for what we were doing," recalled Sommers.

In the course of their daily patrols, the platoon eventually began to befriend people. Sommers frequently would see one of the village elders in the town's small industrial area. He was stunned one day when the Iraqi said, in perfect English, "Hey, how you guys doing?" The elder invited the young lieutenant inside for tea, and the visits became a weekly ritual. "We'd hang out, just two guys, and talk about what's going on, and about the Iraqi soccer team in the Olympics. We felt like we were actually getting through to people."

The Iraqi children had a special place in the hearts of most of the Marines. "I'm fighting for the children, because they are the future," said Private Stokes. Nathan Wood and Derick Lowe played a pickup game of soccer with the kids on a weekly basis. "Hanks always had care packages, squirt guns, balloons, and toys. He was always with kids. This one kid got hit in the head with a rock and stepped on glass. Hanks bandaged his foot, gave him some candy, and sent him on his way," recalled Sojda.

Several of the men tried to learn Arabic, including 3rd Squad's Frank Contreras, who liked to hang out in the Iraqi police station at the edge of town. When one of the Iraqi cops realized Contreras was Latin, he furtively asked, in Spanish, "Puta?" Then, in broken English, he asked, "What does mean?"

"Bitch," Contreras responded, with a hearty laugh. The exchange developed into a friendship, with Contreras teaching the cop Spanish in exchange for Arabic lessons.

First Squad's Sergeant Juan Calderon bonded with the Iraqis through his self-taught, rudimentary Arabic. The villagers fondly called him Juan. Calderon treated the villagers with dignity and respect, and tried to help them with their basic needs. Calderon's sincerity was put to the test when a Humvee from another unit passed through Nasser Wa Salaam one night and accidentally drove through a villager's front yard. During the broiling Iraqi summer, many families sleep on their roofs, or in their front yards, to beat the oppressive heat that lingers into the night. The Humvee nearly killed the sleeping family. When Calderon got word of the incident, he apologized to the family, told them it wouldn't happen again, and promised to return with toys for the children and with food. Calderon did his best to mend fences and win back the trust of the people. The family was impressed.

The improvised explosive device, or IED, was one of the most deadly killers of American troops in Iraq. Typically deployed alongside roads, the bombs were intended to rip apart Coalition troop and supply convoys. IEDs can also be vehicle borne or strapped to the chest of a suicide bomber.

The IED was widely used during the Soviet invasion of Afghanistan, where the mujahideen removed the explosives from Russian land mines and constructed devices they could use in ambushes. The IED is also popular in ambushes against Russian forces in Chechnya.

The degree of sophistication depends on the resources at hand and the skill of the bombmaker. In the first years of the war, IEDs were usually made of old Iraqi mortar rounds or artillery shells. Once the U.S. began to equip more and more vehicles with armor, the mujahideen began to use sophisticated "shaped" explosives. These devices, reportedly imported from Iran, can blast through the side of a tank.

The mujahideen mixed up their tactics, sometimes planting IEDs in stages to make detection and capture more difficult. One man dug the hole, a second planted the charge, and a third man detonated the explosive with a cell phone, garage door opener, or detonator attached to a wire. Contrary to the impression left by media reports, only a small percentage of IED attacks actually inflicted casualties. But when they struck their targets, they were deadly.

During their daily patrols, many of the Marines in the Thundering Third were riding in death traps. The stout, up-armored Humvees that could withstand IED attacks were in short supply. The men had to make do with the vehicles inherited from 1/5 and the equipment they brought with them. Few of the battalion's Humvees were up-armored, though several were equipped with "strike-face" armor:

prefabricated armor kits fitted to the vehicles by Marines in the field. The U.S. military was striving to up-armor all its units in Iraq, but demand far outstripped supply during the summer of 2004. Many of the trucks were fitted with "hillbilly" armor, plates of scrap metal welded to the sides of the vehicles. Hillbilly armor offered only limited protection, but it was better than nothing. Throughout its history, the Marine Corps has had to labor under a limited budget, and often seems to get saddled with the hand-me-downs.

Spotting IEDs was very hit and miss. The men strained their eyes looking for irregularities alongside the road, such as freshly dug earth or a piece of trash that seemed out of place. Some of the men worried themselves to death about IEDs. After going out on dozens of patrols, however, most soldiers and Marines accepted that death in Iraq is random: if your time comes, it comes.

Third Squad encountered its first IED in July. A bomb made of two 155mm artillery shells barely missed Sergeant Conner's vehicle. Spying a suspicious white truck about a mile off, Conner yelled to his men, "Fuck it. We are going after them." Conner pursued the vehicle through the desert for several miles, but the truck's huge head start allowed it to melt away into the Iraq desert. "It was our first brush with death. I stood up to my neck in the hole created by the explosion," recalled Mario Alavez. Nathan Wood, who "never showed any fear," and who was driving Conner's vehicle, put it bluntly: "We cheated death today."

On August 2, Sergeant Juan Calderon, just back from a twelve-hour patrol, volunteered to help run a supply convoy of Humvees from Camp Abu Ghraib to an Iraqi National Guard compound several miles from the prison. Before he left, he challenged Garza to a game of basketball.

"Garza, I'm going to take you on one on one."

"Let's go, Sergeant," replied Garza. "Don't get mad if I beat you."

Staff Sergeant Hackett, who loved competition, chimed in, "He might be good, but I can still beat him."

"I'll be back soon to beat both your asses."

On the way to the CAP India base, Sergeant Calderon's Humvee was hit by an IED. Private First Class Vaquerano recalled "seeing a black cloud," the explosion of the IED, "just before I passed out."

When Vaquerano woke up, he saw Doc Tovar lying next to him inside the stricken Humvee, unconscious.

"Tovar! Tovar!" The corpsman quickly came to.

Three of the four men in the vehicle, Vaquerano, Tovar, and Lance Corporal Bryan, were not badly wounded, but a piece of shrapnel had punched through the windshield and torn away the jaw of the fourth man, Sergeant Calderon. Another Marine in the convoy ran up to the Humvee and said, "Oh, fuck, Sergeant! Stay with us!" Bryan and Tovar both started tending to the mortally wounded sergeant, but the wounds were too severe.

According to Vaquerano, "when I dismounted, I teared up. I was so close to him." Calderon became the platoon's first man lost in its latest deployment to Iraq.

A few hours later, Conner received a knock on the bars of his cell. "Get everyone in the platoon, get them outside," said Staff Sergeant Hackett.

First Platoon reported to the Morale, Welfare, and Recreation Center. With its games and VCR, the rec center provided a place for the Marines to forget about the war for a little bit. The Lima's staff officers were in the room waiting for them.

As the men filed in, Lieutenant Sommers turned to Conner with blank stare and said, "Sergeant Calderon passed away." Staff

Sergeant Hackett sadly lamented, "My only mission was to bring everybody home, and I can't say I did it."

Lima's company commander briefed the men that Sergeant Calderon had been killed by an IED. The men were heartbroken; Calderon was beloved. "All the boots started crying," recalled Sojda. "The first time, when Sledd was killed, I didn't cry. I told them, 'Get used to it, this is the first and it ain't going to be the last.' I wanted them to be ready in case Conner or I went down."

Rage started to boil in the room. One Marine murmured, "Fuck these motherfuckers, kill them all." Conner calmed his men down. "Look, we are going back out there. We can't turn our backs on these people. The mission comes first."

The following day, 1st Platoon returned to Nasser on the daily patrol. Several villagers asked, "Where's Juan?" Conner told them the truth. The patrol made a point of visiting the villager whose family had nearly been killed by the errant Humvee. Again, "Where's Juan?" The Iraqi man was visibly upset by the news of Calderon's death. The Marines delivered the food and toys Calderon had promised to the man, who gratefully accepted the gifts. First Platoon kept Calderon's word.

A few days later, Lieutenant Sommers wrote a painful letter to Sergeant Calderon's unborn son, telling him the father he never knew had died a hero. Sommers's letter was deeply personal, and intended for an audience of one. As the young lieutenant recalls, "I wanted to explain his values, the things that he exhibited as a Marine that defined him as man. These were things that I know Sergeant Calderon would have instilled in his son. Some of them I picked up on just observing him, and listening to his Marines on how he led them; others were things that he flat out said about being a father. I wanted it to be a message from his father, at a time when Juan, Jr. was becoming a man."

4

Trojan Horses

The deadliest weapon in the world is a Marine and his rifle.
—*General John "Black Jack" Pershing*, U.S. Army

A S SUMMER SLOWLY CAME TO AN END, 1st Platoon's missions into Nasser Wa Salaam and other hamlets around the prison became routine. "Nasser got so boring, so repetitive, we got complacent out there," recalled Stokes. As they conducted their twelve-hour missions, the Marines focused on building relationships with the Iraqis. Hanks had his favorite children, as did Conner and most of the other Marines. The exception was Larson. According to Garza, "He isn't much of a kid person. Larson always focused on the enemy, always alert. He never lets his guard down. He told me, 'I'm never going to let anything happen to you,' and I told him the same thing."

The monotony was alleviated a little bit when the platoon found a supply source of a badly missed old friend: alcohol. Unlike Vietnam, where the men could blow off steam and unwind with a cold beer after battle, alcohol consumption for troops serving in Iraq was prohibited. The mess halls all had near beer, but the men viewed the non-alcoholic swill with disdain, so the near beer was left to gather dust in the storage rooms. A few lucky Marines received alcohol in care packages sent by sympathetic relatives or friends. Most caught their first whiff of liquor since June in the traditional Iraqi way—via the black market.

In late August, 1st Platoon got a hot tip about some black marketers from Lima Company's 2nd Platoon. A booze broker approached them during a routine patrol.

"Mister, mister. Beer? Whiskey?" the Iraqi croaked in broken, raspy English.

The stunned Marines responded, "Beer?"

The Iraqi nodded.

"Ah, beer!" Negotiations proceeded in sign language.

For a buck a Marine could buy three or four exotic brews. Eventually, the arrangement grew more sophisticated. The Iraqis would set a time and place, and every couple of weeks, certain members of the platoon picked up the beer. Nathan Wood, always calm, with his obligatory Newport cigarette in hand, remembered that "the Iraqis never failed to deliver."

Once the loot was scored, the Marines needed a secure place to drink it, safe from the prying eyes of officers. Hanks and Sojda's room, the only room in the barracks with a door that locked, became the platoon speakeasy. "We want to play Uno tonight" was the password. With a little ingenuity, the Marines of 1st Platoon found a way to recapture one of the comforts of home.

The party was crashed on September 13th, when the mujahideen attacked the north side of Abu Ghraib Prison with a VBIED (vehicle-borne improvised explosive device). First Platoon's 2nd Squad, on QRF (Quick Reaction Force) duty, spotted a beaten-up car and truck barreling down Route Michigan, the road on the north side of the prison. The terrorist plan called for the suicide bomber driving the car to blow a hole in the prison's outer wall, allowing the anti-aircraft gun in the truck to shoot up the prison's courtyard. Under the command of Sergeant Kyle, 2nd Squad opened fire on the speeding vehicles before they could get near the prison's stone walls. The fusillade of fire detonated the VBIED's eleven 155mm rounds, vaporizing the driver and reducing the car to a tire axle. Second Squad's well-aimed fire halted the truck, forcing several "suspects" to surrender.

The raids on the prison were just a small part of the barrage of attacks directed against the Thundering Third and its parent unit, Regimental Combat Team 1. Every day, the battalion was hit by an IED, mortar, rocket, or sniper. One of the worst attacks fell on September 14th, when the muj launched a rocket attack on RCT-1's headquarters. Aimed from several miles away, the rocket ripped through the headquarters building with pinpoint accuracy, killing the regiment's communications officer, Lieutenant Colonel Kevin Shea. RCT-1's commanding officer, Colonel Nicholsen, was severely wounded and evacuated to the United States. He was replaced by forty-five-year-old Colonel Michael Shupp.

In mid-September, the platoon received word that locals were stealing metal from a scrapyard in Nasser Wa Salaam. The Marines set up an inner-outer cordon on the night of September 18th to stop any looters and search carts for purloined metal. Sergeant. Kyle's 2nd Squad maintained the outer cordon, while Conner's 3rd Squad held the inner cordon. As the night wore on, Kyle's Marines stopped several carts and turned over looters to the local police. Then a horse-drawn cart carrying two Iraqis broke through Kyle's cordon and bore down on 3rd Squad. The driver was whipping the horse, making it gallop faster and faster. Lengths of rebar metal dangled over the sides of the cart, hitting the ground and creating a shower of white sparks. The cart almost ran over two Marines, Lowe and Huyett.

The men recognized that the cart posed a serious threat. Several days earlier a Marine had been killed and four others wounded by a VBIED hidden in a donkey cart. The dangling pieces of rebar, swinging like rapiers, could easily decapitate a Marine or civilian. The cart's driver looked like he was trying to grab something, and the men thought it could be a weapon.

"Stop!"

"Auguff!"

"Halt!"

"Stop!"

"Stop, Mother Fucker!"

Nothing seemed to get the driver's attention as the cart hurtled on through the darkness. The Marines fired a warning shot, but the cart kept coming. When it drew within thirty feet, 3rd Squad reluctantly opened fire. Mario Alavez remembers the incident. "I was carrying a SAW and another Marine was in front of me with an M16. I was ready to fill the driver with lead. *Pop, pop, pop,* one of the other Marines opened fire. The dude slammed into the side of a house. That was the first time I saw somebody get killed and I remember thinking 'what a dumb son of a bitch.'" The Marines had no choice but to shoot when the driver failed to heed their warnings.

"Back off!" barked Conner.

"It could be an IED!" shouted one of the Marines.

After waiting a few minutes the Marines approached the wreckage. The driver had been killed by a bullet that traveled under his armpit and into his heart, while the other Iraqi was wounded in the thigh.

First Platoon's twenty-five-year-old Corpsman Oliver "Doc" Escanilla, a native of the Philippines, scrambled to treat the wounded Iraqi. Remarkably, it was the man's second gunshot wound to the same area. The Iraqi was either a former soldier in Saddam's armed forces or a muj.

As Escanilla bandaged up the Iraqi, the platoon heard the loud crackle of an American .50 caliber machine gun. White-orange tracer rounds streaked through the darkness and lit up the area around them.

"What the fuck!" shouted Conner.

Hearing the shots and believing they were under fire, a nearby Marine AAV unit opened up on 1st Platoon. Illumination rounds turned the night into day as fire poured into the village; the fuckup, which could have caused friendly fire casualties, nearly resulted in another civilian death. An Iraqi woman was wounded by a stray .50 caliber round.

"We were pissed, all that hard [SASO] work and they shot up the place. We had to rebuild the trust. So we apologized and told them it was an Army unit that opened fire on the village. We said 'Army crazy' to anyone who asked about that night," recalled Conner.

For Sommers and the boots, it was their first experience with killing. Tragically, the men in the cart were most likely just average Iraqis trying to get home with their looted scrap metal—but no one knew for sure.

Perhaps the most difficult aspect of the war in Iraq is distinguishing friend from foe. The Thundering Third's Marines were training two Iraqi National Guard units, Combined Action Patrol (CAP) India and CAP Delta. CAP India was largely successful and would later fight alongside Lima Company. CAP Delta, on the other hand, was a disaster. In Delta's case, the fish stank at the head. Delta's commanding officer and his brother, were tied to the mujahideen. On September 18th, a raid launched by RCT-1's new commanding officer, Colonel Mike Shupp, snared both individuals. Days earlier, one of 3/1's most beloved interpreters, Hadji Kamil, had been gunned down in Baghdad "by men believed to have been led by one of the Battalion's previous fired interpreters, a man suspected of providing information to the insurgents regarding Battalion activities," 3/1's command chronology notes. Clearly, the muj's secret networks and intimidation tactics were extensive and effective.

In an attempt to "deter and disrupt" enemy hijacking and intimidation activities, Lima Company conducted clandestine operations in the vicinity of Abu Ghraib Prison on September 22–23. The mission started with a "Trojan Horse" operation, a follow-up to a campaign begun on July 11, with the Scout Sniper Platoon carrying out missions "designed to deceive the enemy . . . the operations utilized captured indigenous vehicles and partial disguises."

In an effort to gather intelligence or covertly insert snipers into ambush positions, several members of 1st Platoon, mostly Hispanics, who had the best chance to pass as Middle Easterners, were issued Iraqi clothing to wear over their uniforms. Nineteen-year-old Lance Corporal Craig James III, 2nd Squad's stocky, African-American, self-proclaimed "hustler" from Chicago, was morphed into a Somalian. James was joined by Corporal Abudayeh, whose language skills were very helpful during operations.

Battalion after-action reports assert that "the enemy had no idea the operations were occurring." However, some Americans had their doubts about Trojan Horse. "You have to be shitting me; none of the Mexicans even have to shave," opined Conner.

In the September 25 operation, James was placed in the trunk of a battered red Opel to snap pictures of intelligence targets. The vehicle's trunk was armored and outfitted with a moveable license plate peephole for James's camera. If things went south, James also had an M16 and a shotgun. James, the first in his family to join the military, grinned while describing the experience. "Just call me Lee Malvo. It was a sweat box; I didn't have nothing on me but shorts and a tee shirt."

In a disastrous oversight, some Marines from another company hadn't been informed that the red Opel was friendly. When the car got too close to their vehicle, they opened fire with an automatic weapon, slightly wounding Corporal Abudayeh. Though 1st Platoon snared nine mujahideen during the operation, the friendly fire incident sounded the death knell for the Trojan Horse campaign, and also allegedly led to the removal of Lima Company's commanding officer.

Lima Company quickly received a new commander, thirty-two-year-old Captain Brian Heatherman. The San Diego native joined the Corps out of family tradition. His entire family had been in military service, including his eldest brother, who served as a Marine platoon leader in Vietnam. Heatherman was a veteran of the Marine Special Operations training group, was airborne qualified, and was one of the few Marines who had graduated from the U.S. Army Ranger School.

Hanks was intrigued by Heatherman's Ranger training. Lima's first sergeant, who had killed the terrorists on Failaka Island, introduced the two men. Only days earlier, Hanks had reenlisted for another four years in the Corps.

"Sir, I want you to meet Lance Corporal Hanks. He is really motivated, and wants to go to Ranger School. When it comes to the field he totally has his shit together. He just loves this shit. I know you've been there, could you tell him what it takes to make it through Ranger School? He just reenlisted."

Heatherman told Hanks that of his Ranger class of 295 Army recruits and five Marines, only fifty men, including two Marines, had graduated. Ranger School is one of the U.S. Army's most difficult training courses, considered a prerequisite for the majority of their Special Forces.

"What's your PFT (Physical Fitness Test) score?" asked Heatherman.

"225," responded Hanks.

"The bare minimum. You need to bring your A Game and get in shape. Ranger School is 90 percent mental and 10 percent physical. I'll help you get ready," said Heatherman in an upbeat tone. Hanks had decided to make the Marine Corps his career, and Heatherman intended to encourage him. The new CO was a breath of fresh air for Lima Company.

5

Feints

We signed up knowing the risk. Those innocent people in
New York didn't go to work thinking there was any kind of risk.
—*Private Mike Armendariz-Clark*, USMC; Afghanistan,
September 20, 2001

AS HE STUDIED THE EMPTY GAS STATION THROUGH HIS
night vision goggles, Sergeant Bennie Conner stamped his
feet to get rid of the shivers running through his body. With the
onset of fall, Iraq turns cold at night, a bone-numbing cold. As September drew to a close, the nights and days and operations seemed
to blend into each other. Memories of the various "ops" were blurry,
because in most cases nothing happened. First Platoon's duties
were less combat than police work.

Tonight's patrol would turn out more memorable than the others. Third Squad was looking to ambush any insurgents planting
IEDs on Route Michigan, a main supply road that ran past Camp
Abu Ghraib to Baghdad. The Leprechaun deployed his men on a
tiny slope that overlooked a gas station on Route Michigan. The station was always busy during the day, but closed at night. A thick
stand of tall grass lay in front of the squad, so Conner moved up and

down the line, pushing his Marines deeper into the grass to get a better view of their target. The wind blew gently on their faces as they crept through the tall strands of dry foliage. The night was quiet, except for the occasional dog's bark. Radio silence was broken by Hanks's laughter over the radio.

"You aren't going to believe this."

"What's wrong?" replied Conner.

"Larson just fell into shit up to his head."

Private First Class Nick Larson had slipped into a massive pool of animal excrement collected by one of the local farmers. With the entire squad laughing, even Larson, normally the strong silent type, chuckled at his predicament.

As October approached, 1st Platoon was still providing security around Abu Ghraib Prison and conducting SASO operations in Fallujah's suburbs. The enemy in 1st Platoon's sector remained unseen, like ghosts, while the local population seemed mostly friendly, at least during the day. As in Vietnam, distinguishing between friend and foe was a constant challenge.

In contrast to 1st Platoon, whose area of operation was relatively calm, the rest of the Thundering Third was tormented incessantly by IEDs, ambushes, and rocket attacks. Fallujah had become the biggest staging area in the country for the mujahideen. According to Lieutenant Colonel Buhl, jihadists "sallied out from Fallujah and attacked us every day." The battalion's Command Chronology reveals the situation faced by the Marines: "The enemy, at this point, was fully established and operating in his safe haven of the city of al-Fallujah. He had steadily increased his operational capabilities over the past six months since the failed political settlement of Operation Vigilant Resolve [the aborted attack on the city by Coalition forces in April]. At this point he was able to conduct multiple coordinated attacks all around the city of al-Fallujah . . ."

While they were stepping up their attacks against the Marines, the muj were also busy turning Fallujah into a fortress.

Every day, jihadists from around the world were traveling via "rat lines," a series of safe houses that stretched from Syria into Fallujah. The so-called insurgency inside the city was more than just a home-grown opposition movement. In reality, it was a motley assortment of "foreign fighters, criminal elements, Islamofascists, former Baathists, former regime elements who want to return to the days of Saddam, and Islamists who don't want to see democracy in Iraq," according to Lieutenant Colonel Scott Shuster, plans officer for 1st Marine Division. Foreign fighters from no fewer than eighteen different countries played significant roles in the defense of Fallujah. Entire companies of Jordanians, Syrians, and Saudis were posted in the southern portion of the city. Seasoned Islamist fighters from Chechnya were spread in ones and twos throughout Fallujah. Because they were dispersed, the Marines inferred that they were training their comrades, passing along the expertise gained while fighting the Russian army in the brutal battle for Grozny. The city's defenders swelled to somewhere between seven and ten thousand strong.

The mujahideen dug trenches throughout the city, deployed numerous IEDs, and converted thousands of Fallujah's 39,000 buildings into bunkers. They used nearly half of the city's mosques, along with most of the hospitals and schools, as supply dumps or strong points. "In one mosque, every room contained different munitions, rockets in this room, mortars in that room, machine gun rounds in that room. Mosques were used as fighting positions or to store weapons. Yet God forbid I should attack the building, or it's on the news that the Marines desecrated a mosque," recalled one senior Marine.

According to America's usual rules of engagement, buildings like mosques and hospitals are supposed to lose their immunity when they are put to military use; yet the political leadership above the Marines refused to allow these targets to be attacked. "On the Marine Expeditionary Force level, we had all kinds of targets we wanted to prosecute. MNFI (Multi-National Forces-Iraq) would not clear the fires." As one senior Marine put it, there was an "unwillingness of senior commanders outside the Marine Corps to employ all of our assets, out of concern for the information operations threshold—the potential for insurgents to exploit collateral damage in the media."

Absurdly, RCT-1 (Regimental Combat Team 1, which included 3/1) was not allowed to adequately soften up enemy defensive positions before the assault with "preparatory fires," or bombardments by planes and artillery, until they were fired upon by the mujahideen inside Fallujah. The civilian leadership and the Pentagon brass were so fearful of inflicting excessive civilian casualties that they tied the hands of the commanders on the ground with questionable rules of engagement, putting the lives of Coalition soldiers at risk. A Marine with intimate knowledge of the air bombardment said, "Only about thirty shaping attacks [to destroy bunkers and enemy positions] took place when about three hundred were needed." As the battle raged, a senior officer observed, "Blood is on someone's hands."

What the CIA and Pentagon brass did not know, or at least did not acknowledge in their orders until a day or so, after the attack began, was that hardly any civilians remained in Fallujah. The Marines had been ordered to draw up contingency plans for dealing with 15,000 displaced civilians, but the great majority had heeded weeks of warnings from the U.S. military to flee the city.

Because of the political constraints, the mujahideen were able to build trenches and berms with impunity. They even conducted indirect training in broad daylight. "We saw them practicing with indirect fire, mortars, but we weren't allowed to shoot. We could not get clearance," recalled Lieutenant Colonel Shuster.

Once again the "insurgents" seemed to take advantage of a paradigm shift on how war is now fought. Some military experts argue that the entire world has become a battlefield. The human element and world opinion has become paramount and can shape a conflict. The fulcrum for this shift is the global media which through its reporting can influence world opinion. Single events such as the Abu Ghraib Prison scandal or the accidental bombings of civilians in Lebanon can change the course of an entire conflict. Tragically, our troops are often caught in the middle of the politics.

At the highest levels, diplomats were still seeking a political solution to the Fallujah problem. Negotiations between the interim Iraqi government and the mujahideen in Fallujah continued into October, culminating in mid-October with Secretary of Defense Donald Rumsfeld flying to Baghdad. Iyad Allawi, interim Iraqi prime minister, told Fallujah's ruling council, the Shura, to hand over Zarqawi and all foreign fighters. They refused. As the talks dragged on, precious time was lost, and the mujahideen continued to gain strength. Finally, at the end of October, the provisional government and the Coalition forces gave up on the negotiations, and decided to send in the Marines.

Fallujah promised to be an urban battle of epic proportions. Every single one of the city's 400,000 rooms would have to be cleared, bulldozed, or blown to pieces. The assault plan for the city called for six battalions of Coalition forces, about seven thousand American and Iraqi troops, to strike the city from the north. Assaults normally require a three-to-one numerical advantage; but in one of the few instances in modern warfare, the defenders in Fallujah would outnumber the attackers. In 3/1's case, the defenders had at least a two-to-one advantage over the attackers. The strategists planning the battle were counting on the U.S. military's ability to concentrate its superior firepower, technology, and troops at any given point on the battlefield, while forcing the defenders to remain dispersed. American dominance of the air space over Fallujah would make it difficult for the mujahideen to maneuver their troops or concentrate in units greater than platoon strength. As Lieutenant Colonel Shuster put it, the plan relied on "pitting three hundred Marines against a single enemy platoon."

Fallujah's defenders enjoyed a number of advantages in addition to numerical superiority. The dense city concealed their locations. They were on home turf, and had many places to hide and prepare ambushes. The rugged urban terrain would negate important elements of America's high-tech digital technology. For example, online maps wouldn't work inside the city, forcing the troops to rely on radios. Above all, the mujahideen had months to train and to prepare their defenses.

Mujahideen training consisted primarily of studying the Koran and learning how to handle weapons. Much of the training was conducted indoors, in large warehouses, sheltered from the watchful eyes of American spy satellites and unmanned aerial vehicles (UAVs). Muj pamphlets taught fighters to defeat U.S. body armor by aiming for the side of the vest, between the ceramic plates, or by aiming at the face. Manuals described how to make IEDs, and how to conceal objects inside vehicles, so that ambulances could be used to transport men and ammunition. For many of the jihadists, the focus was to prepare men to kill an American and martyr themselves in the process.

While the mujahideen were getting ready to do battle, the Marines were training intensively as well. Conner made his men build a schoolhouse out of sandbags and scrap wood to serve as 3rd Squad's private lesson center for house clearing and urban warfare. Conner wanted a sanctuary, a place where his squad could come together undisturbed to brush up on their combat skills. It was also the squad's last teambuilding exercise. As Derick Lowe recalled, "Initially, we just put some benches out. That didn't cut it; he wanted a roof and everything. We had to tear it down and redo it until we finally had it the way he wanted it."

Inside the sandbag schoolhouse, the men practiced clearing houses, casualty evacuation techniques, and the other urban combat skills. The men never had a break. "With the other squads there was a lot of off time, but we were always training or teaching each other classes inside the schoolhouse. Conner prepared us for combat and nothing else," recalled Derick Lowe.

Clearing rooms remained the focus of Conner's training. Back in the States, some of the men initially hesitated before entering a room. "After we threw in the practice grenade, sometimes you'd have to nudge them into the freaking room," recalled Sojda. Now, most of the Marines controlled their fear and were ready to lay down their lives for their brothers in arms.

"Garza, if you had a choice between you or Larson getting killed, who would you rather see die?" asked Sodja.

"I would rather die than see Larson killed," Garza responded with a straight face.

"Good. That's brotherhood," remarked Sojda.

The training in the schoolhouse continued:

"Conner brought us all together and all we did was MOUT; we cleared a house for about two hours. At about 10:30 that night he had us breach a door with a sledgehammer and clear rooms," recalled Lowe.

To further toughen his Marines, Conner made his men carry twenty-pound sandbags in their combat packs everywhere they went, even to the chow hall. The move caused consternation among the grunts. "We were walking around like stupid motherfuckers," recalled one of 3rd Squad's Marines. This "tough love" was Conner's way of developing mental toughness in his Marines, to give them the edge.

Lima's first test under Captain Heatherman was to stage a feint attack outside the city on October 18th. Feints were intended to keep the insurgents guessing about which direction the main assault would come from, and to draw defenders away from the actual path of the assault in the north. During the exercise, 1st Platoon, much to the disappointment of the men, stayed behind to guard the area around the prison. "We thought we would never get into the battle, that our job might just be guarding the prison. It seemed like 2nd Platoon was going on all the cool missions. We wanted to see what Fallujah looked like, since we had been hearing about it since April," recalled Conner. The men felt let down.

First Platoon's first real taste of fire came on October 21, when Lima Company conducted another feint attack. In Operation Black Bear II, Lima Company, reinforced by a sniper team, a mortar section, assaultmen, tanks, and engineers, rolled out of Camp Abu Ghraib to probe the defenses on the eastern side of Fallujah. The feint provided useful information to the Marines.

"Had we decided to attack from the south, the battle would have been hellacious from day one," recalled Conner. "The thing we discovered after the battle was that they oriented a lot of their defenses to the south."

Muj resistance was intense. According to Conner, "one tank ran over a mine. Mortar rounds were coming in pretty close, close enough that the track we were in rocked back and forth from the concussion."

Cooped up in their troop carrier as if they were in the belly of a dimly lit submarine, most of 3rd Squad was itching to get into the fight.

"This is bullshit, why are we just sitting here? Let's get out and do something," said Sojda.

"If they want to play, let's play," snapped Hanks.

Lima Company drew a lot of fire from the mujahideen during the operation, but nobody was hit. From a tactical perspective, the company experienced teething pains getting everyone into attack positions. However, the operation provided a valuable dress rehearsal before the real attack. After a few hours, Lima withdrew from the engagement and returned to Camp Abu Ghraib, much to the chagrin of some of the men.

"This is bullshit. Since when do Marines retreat from a fight?" griped Hanks. The bellicose lance corporal was speaking for most of the platoon. Out of patriotism, sheer boredom, and a desire to avenge lost comrades, 1st Platoon was itching for a fight. "All we wanted to do was start hooking and jabbing," recalled Conner. The men handled themselves well; outwardly, at least, no one flinched from the exposure to indirect fire.

Throughout the remainder of October, Fallujah's terrorists harassed the battalion on a daily basis. Mortars and rockets hit Camp Abu Ghraib, and several Marines were wounded by VBIEDs. The insurgents launched their most dangerous IED attack on October 23, when the battalion commanding officer Willie Buhl's convoy was struck by a "platter charge" IED mounted on the back of a bicycle. A platter charge IED consists of plastic explosive sandwiched between two pieces of flat metal. The plastic propels the metal platter into the target. The device is capable of penetrating an up-armored Humvee. The attack wounded four Americans, including the intelligence officer for the U.S. Army's 1/5 Cavalry Battalion, who was inspecting the area before his unit took over the al-Karmah and Shahabi areas of operation. The attack was the ultimate eye-opener for the army battalion commander and his staff, who received a firsthand introduction to the dangers of Fallujah.

One of the deadliest outposts outside the gates of Camp Abu Ghraib was the Delta Iraqi National Guard base. Third Squad's close friend, Sergeant Greg Smith, a sniper who frequently deployed with 1st Platoon, was assigned to Delta on the evening of October 25th. As the sun was going down, Smith and his spotter were going over their next mission, checking their maps and drawing out the mission in the sand, when the mujahideen launched a devastating attack. "We heard a high pitched scream," recalled Smith. "A 122mm rocket came sailing over our heads. A tenth of a second before it hit, it illuminated the Marines standing next to me. It blasted Corporal Brian Olivera, who moments earlier was showing pictures of his newborn baby boy, and blew me backwards against the wall. Dust was everywhere, so thick you couldn't see your own hand. I stood up, and after trying to catch my breath, I looked down and warm blood was pouring down my fingers. I felt my chest, it was bleeding. There was a hole where my collar bone was supposed to be. It was ripped open. I put my hand inside the hole created by the shrapnel. It felt like worms moving around inside there." The rocket hit the center of Delta's compound, wounding fourteen Marines and killing Olivera.

Smith's collarbone was vaporized by the rocket. He almost died from blood loss when his wounds reopened during the helicopter ride to Baghdad. After surgery in Baghdad and Germany, Smith was sent home. The flight to the United States should have been a comfort, but in the plane Smith experienced an overpowering dose of the horror of war. "They put us in the back of a C-17. The back of the plane contained hooks for all the stretchers. They were all fully loaded with the wounded from Iraq and Afghanistan. They started hanging Marines; people were screaming in agony and pain. They were hanging from the ceiling all the way down to the floor. The nurses were giving people injections, running back and forth. I looked up. The guy above me was missing half his head. The nurse was trying to comfort him, and she said she had to go since they were losing someone in the front of the plane. She ran up to help him, the flight nurses were amazing. I was in a lot of pain. As I looked up blood was dripping down on my face from the man in the stretcher above me. I remember the faces of the guys. That stays with you."

6

The Die Is Cast

Theirs not to make reply,
Theirs but to do or die.
—*Alfred Lord Tennyson*,
"The Charge of the Light Brigade"

"I WANT TO THANK YOU FROM THE COUNTRY AND THE MARINE Corps for the job you have done here in Iraq. . . ."

On the afternoon of November 5, the entire Thundering Third assembled on the "grinder," a dusty open area near the battalion's command post at Camp Abu Ghraib. Each company in the approximately one thousand-man battalion silently stood facing the others in a rectangular formation. The battalion's battle guidons, along with the George Company guidon that survived the Frozen Chosin in Korea, fluttered in the light breeze, as the blazing Iraqi sun beat down on the Marines. Colonel Michael Shupp, the new CO of RCT-1, confidently addressed the men. Shupp clarified the rules of engagement (ROE) to make it understood that the rules were different inside the city. ROEs were often a thorny issue in Iraq.

"When you go into a fight, you fight for each other. You fight for your fellow Marines. Those are the things that really matter. You have the right to protect yourself . . . Take the fight to the enemy, but fight with firmness, dignity, and respect. You are warriors, not criminals."

The charismatic regimental commander moved on to discuss the historical significance of the forthcoming battle. "This is one of our largest fights since Vietnam. As time goes by, when we celebrate the Marine Corps birthday, Fallujah will be just as significant as the battle for Inchon, the Chosin Reservoir, Khe Sanh, or Hue City. It will ring in Marine Corps history as another great epic battle we fought in war." Shupp brought the significance of the battle down to a personal level. "One day, when we go to the Marine Corps ball or a pageant, Fallujah will be something that you remember for the rest of your lives. Over the next forty-eight hours, the entire world will be watching you."

Shupp was part of a long list of individuals who addressed the Marines before the battle. "Everyone and their brother wanted to say their piece," recalled Sommers, including one speaker who bluntly stated, "Do your worst. Kill everything in front of you."

The speakers broadly outlined the battalion's role in the battle. Without being told the details, the Marines were informed that the main assault force would be composed of six American battalions and several hundred Iraqi National Guard troops, and that 3/1 would play a crucial role in the Coalition assault, physically occupying the heart of the mujahideen defenses. According to Wade, "They said it was going to be a seventeen-hour battle and we'd be done. I never would have imagined it turned out the way it did." Finally, several speakers informed the men the first rows of buildings into the city would be demolished by air and artillery and the battle was going to be brief.

Nearly everyone in the platoon considered the speeches highly "moto." Stokes remembered "getting chills, being all motivated. I made peace with God in case I died." Wade wasn't sure about the historical significance of the battle. "I turned to my best friend, Lance Corporal Nathan Wood, and I said, 'I don't know.' I remember Wood then said, 'I don't think it's going to be that big.' I recalled how many Marines were glorified in places like Hue City and Chosin Reservoir, and I didn't see Fallujah as being up there."

Bill Sojda's thoughts on the speakers were more pragmatic. *"The bottom line is we knew we are going. They don't give speeches like that unless we are going to attack."*

Shortly after the pep talks, 1st Platoon's enlisted men shuffled back to their temporary barracks outside the camp, passing signs painted on plywood, "REMEMBER OP SEC" (operational security) and "COMPLACENCY KILLS!" Sommers and the other company officers, including Lima Company commander Captain Brian Heatherman, filed into 3/1's command post, a gray stone building in the middle of Camp Abu Ghraib. One of the CP's rooms contained a massive sand table that graphically displayed enemy bunkers and defensive positions throughout the entire city. On the table, the men worked through the battle plan for the first forty-eight hours of Operation Al-Fajr (New Dawn, initially code-named Operation Phantom Fury). Plastic model tanks and figures represented Coalition units down to the company level. Every officer with a role in the battle had to brief the entire audience by picking up the model representing his respective unit and physically walking the model over the table.

The command briefing began with video footage from a Dragon Eye, a tiny remote controlled unmanned aerial vehicle (UAV) that provided live images of the battlefield. Dragon Eye, in theory, would give the Marines a bird's eye view of their immediate battle space. Fallujah was Dragon Eye's debut in a major urban battle. The UAVs would prove to be crucial assets, continuously providing information about enemy troop movements to company commanders.

"The Dragon Eye footage of the city was clear as my mom's video camera," recalled Heatherman. "We viewed the whole city, seeing what we were about to fight through. All the houses we had to clear. I remembered thinking to myself, 'Wow, this place is huge.'"

The video identified muj fighting positions and even black-clad jihadists on the roofs of buildings firing at the little UAV as it flew by. The video panned from Fallujah's train station to the water treatment plant, Lima Company's first objective.

"Holy crap! That's a lot of houses, they're all bunched together, and we don't have the tanks, dozers, or other assets the other company had; we just have Marines. That's over 1,500 meters to the water treatment plant; there's hundreds of houses, and each one has to be cleared," thought Heatherman.

As Jeff Sommers peered down on the enormous 50 x 50 sand table, studying the massive force surrounding the city, he was thinking, "This is finally it. We have been waiting months for this thing."

Dubbed Task Force Fallujah, the Coalition assault force numbered approximately 7,000 troops. Surrounding the city was the Army's Blackjack Brigade, consisting of a number of units, including 1/5 Cavalry and the attached Marine special operations-like unit, 2nd Recon Battalion. The assault forces were divided into two regiments.

Regimental Combat Team 1 (RCT-1) consisted of the 3rd Battalion, 1st Marines (3/1); 3rd Battalion, 5th Marines (3/5); the Army's 2nd Battalion, 7th Cavalry (2/7); and a smaller, attached unit, 3rd Light Armored Reconnaissance Battalion (3rd LAR). Regimental Combat Team 7 (RCT-7) consisted of 1st Battalion, 8th Marines (1/8); 1st Battalion, Third Marines (1/3); and the Army's 2nd Battalion, 2nd Infantry Regiment (2/2). Spec Ops troops, support units, and U.S.-trained Iraqi units also entered the mix.

The Coalition battle plan called for the six main assault battalions and supporting Iraqi troops to hit the northern edge of the city and push south. 3/1 would play the crucial role of driving through the heart of the city's defenses, the Jolan neighborhood—and hooking west toward the Euphrates River—pushing the muj into a kill zone.

After several officers gave their briefings, Heatherman took his turn at the table. Picking up the figure representing his company, Lima's CO confidently walked through Lima's plan for the first forty-eight hours of the battle. Lima would lead 3/1 into the city, initially by supporting an assault on Fallujah's train station by an Iraqi National Guard unit and a platoon of Marines and Iraqis from the Combined Action Platoon known as CAP India. Once the train station was secure, Lima would enter the edge of the city to provide supporting fire for a platoon of combat engineers creating breach lanes for 2/7's tanks. The armor was to penetrate nearly a mile into the city, to a road dubbed Phase Line Elizabeth, overrunning the muj defenses and cutting off reinforcements to the front line. The Thundering Third would follow the armor and perform the toughest task, taking possession of the real estate. Lima would clear the muj out of all buildings between the train station and the water treatment plant.

"The momentum of the fight will carry us through. This train is moving south come hell or high water," thought Heatherman. In retrospect, Heatherman conceded: "I don't think any of us really knew how to fight through those houses until we did it."

Later, Heatherman briefed Lima's men on their upcoming role in Operation Al-Fajr (New Dawn). After the briefing, 1st Platoon prepared for battle: the men cleaned their weapons, made last minute equipment checks, and mentally prepared for a fight they could only imagine in their minds' eyes. Most of the men took a shower, knowing it might be their last for days. Word filtered down to the platoon: "we are going tonight." But it was a false alarm, the first of several. "We didn't know when we were going. They kept rolling back the date. Several nights we were told we were going and it didn't happen for whatever reason," recalled Bennie Conner. The anticipation wore on everyone's nerves, causing some of the Marines to crave combat, to alleviate the boredom, or at least finish the job so they could go home.

Besides preparing for the battle, the platoon still had mundane tasks to perform. Once a week, Sommers assigned two Marines and one NCO to return to Camp Abu Ghraib for security detail. When Private First Class Nicholas Larson was assigned the thankless duty, Bennie Conner, Sergeant Kyle, and Hanks decided to play a joke on the twenty-year-old private—but the joke served mostly to demonstrate the strength of Larson's character.

"Larson," said Conner. "You aren't going into Fallujah, since you're not going to get back in time." Disappointment registered all over Larson's face.

"Larson, why do you want to go to Fallujah?" snapped Hanks. "At least you're not gonna take the chance of getting shot or killed."

"It's going to be an in-and-out job; we'll be back before you know it," said Conner.

Larson looked at Hanks with a straight face. "I'd rather take the chance to get shot and killed than not go with the platoon."

Everyone let the joke ride for a few minutes, until Conner and Hanks broke out laughing. "You'll be back in time for the fight. Now get to work."

A few hours later, back in the main compound of Camp Abu Ghraib, Sommers and Gunny Hackett pulled Larson off guard duty and promoted him from private first class to lance corporal.

"I never saw him have any emotion at all. When we pinned lance corporal on him, he was smiling and happy. I took pictures of the event, I always made a point of doing that, but unfortunately they never came out," recalled Sommers. Larson pulled security for a few days, and rejoined the platoon shortly before the battle.

Once the entire platoon was together again, all forty-five members of 1st Platoon took one last photo together. Standing in a long line outside the sandy tan barracks, many of the Marines were wearing new uniforms that in just days would be grimy, torn, and spattered with blood. If you look at the eyes of any one of the Marines, and compare them to a picture of the same person taken before the war, you will see the toll five months in Iraq had taken from them, even before the battle.

"Pack up your shit, we are rolling!" At 0020 on November 8, word finally came down for 1st Platoon and the rest of the battalion to move out of Camp Abu Ghraib and assemble in their attack positions outside the northwest part of the city. Conner's men piled like sardines into tracks commanded by Staff Sergeant Russell Slay, and rolled forward. There are no windows in the tracks, and men riding in them are tossed from side to side. Unless they look out the open hatch, they lose sense of direction and space. Blue cigarette smoke quickly filled the tub-like interior of the tracks. The interiors of the tracks are spartan, and the men feel every bump on the way to the staging area.

Sergeant Conner brought two favorite keepsakes into the battle, a replica "Don't Tread on Me" flag from the American Revolution, and a grimy white baseball cap embroidered with an orange longhorn, labeled "Texas," that he attached to the back of his body armor.

Some units in the convoy took fire as they left the gate. "From that point on there was no laughing, the faces on my men changed to strictly business. There was no emotion; some people were praying, 'God let me get through this, I'll never do this and that again, etc.,'" one Marine attached to Lima Company described it.

The bumpy ride lasted about an hour. The men dismounted and moved into positions along berms and small hills on the northern part of the city near the battalion's first objective, Fallujah's train station. The plan called for the station to be captured intact, because its location and reinforced concrete walls made it an ideal command center and field hospital.

When his track reached the top of the highest hills, Conner looked back at the columns of vehicles, which stretched for miles. "Tanks were staged out there. The amtracks were staged. The other platoon Humvees were staged, ready to go."

After reaching their staging position, the platoon tried to dig foxholes in the rocky knolls. While the men were attacking the rock with their entrenching tools, barely scratching the surface, Conner brought out his Walkman and a tiny pair of speakers, and 3rd Squad listened to songs like "I Love this Bar" and the "The Taliban Song" by Toby Keith. The men made last minute checks of their gear, and many prayed that they would return home.

"Everybody tried to dig in, into the back side of this hill. It's rock hard. We spent all night trying to dig in. We kept beating the side of the hill and we hardly put a dent in it for our fighting holes. Eventually, we gave up trying to make fighting holes. Next, it starts raining, it's dark and ominous. People start sliding down the hill. I thought to myself, 'I can't believe it's raining.' That night I reflected on everything we had done in the past, all the stuff at the prison, or Nasser Wa Salaam. I felt comfortable with my team. I knew they weren't going to let me down. We were tight, very tight," remembered Lance Corporal Mario Alavez. "Meanwhile, jets were flying over, gunning it with their cannons, blowing shit up. We were watching it; it was awesome, awesome. We couldn't sleep and were riveted just watching it. I remember thinking there isn't going to be anything left when we go in there."

Jets, helicopters, and AC-130U gunships continued to target enemy positions inside the city. Blue tracers arced down like lightning from the AC-130U into muj targets. The AC-130Us dominated the battlefield. The planes were flying arsenals, armed with a 105mm howitzer, a 40mm Bofors cannon, and multiple 25mm chain or Gatling guns. Against the backdrop of the plane's deep, intimidating, B-17-like drone, the weapons emitted their own haunting screeches. The AC-130Us became "the most feared weapons of the enemy, the enemy was terrified of that weapons system," according to a senior Marine who coordinated the planes' missions. "The enemy would react to it, either by stopping moving or starting to move. We could use the aircraft to make the enemy react. We would use it in deceptions and for all kinds of different operations."

One of the AC-130Us, known as Basher, was a huge morale booster. "I'd fuck that plane if it was a woman, I love it that much," joked one of the Marines. Most of the men didn't realize Basher was indeed commanded by a female Air Force officer. Her superb performance saved countless lives.

The morning of November 8th passed uneventfully for the platoon, but in midafternoon, Heatherman ordered 2nd and 3rd Squads to sweep a series of farmhouses near the platoon's attack position on the hill. The sweep was a nonevent. Conner's men found a couple of "bolt action rifles and an SKS or AK." Otherwise the buildings were empty. Apparently the farmers fled, realizing they were too close to the fray.

As Task Force Fallujah finalized its movement into attack positions, 3rd LAR kicked off RCT-1's offensive with an attack up a peninsula formed by the Euphrates River on the west side of the city. Third LAR's mission was to secure the Fallujah Hospital and the two bridges leading out of the city. The hospital was an important target. During the first battle for the city, it was used by the muj to grossly exaggerate civilian casualties for propaganda purposes.

Simultaneously, the Army's Blackjack Brigade tightened the ring around the southern part of the city, sealing escape routes. Fallujah's dam bridge was secured by 2nd Recon and a platoon of Bradley Infantry Fighting Vehicles from B Company, 1/5. The Marine and Army units executed their tasks flawlessly, smashing the enemy resistance holding the bridges and the hospital.

The assault on the city began at 1100 on November 8, with 3/5 seizing a large apartment complex. The apartments overlooked the "route of attack" lanes and were needed as a staging area for new units and personnel heading into the city. Conner's squad had a bird's eye view of the opening act in the battle as Marines stormed the apartments.

"Fuck just sitting here!" Conner begged Sommers for permission to accompany a sniper team being sent over to the berm overlooking the apartments about 500 meters away from their positions.

"We scanned the area looking for targets of opportunity. We were trying to tell who was Marine and who wasn't," recalled Conner.

Bill Sojda recalled the assault: "I could see the Marines roll up and take the apartment complex down. Tracers, a lot of arty (artillery), and Willy Pete (white phosphorous) came down outside the complex. I guess people were coming out." Back on the berm, the platoon heard the screams from the dying fighters inside the buildings.

"Man, that gives me a hard-on," quipped one of 1st Platoon's Marines. The platoon was finally getting a chance to take the fight to the invisible enemy—the same enemy who planted IEDs, dropped mortar shells, or conducted hit and run ambushes, but never fought them in a pitched battle.

In the midst of the assault, Sojda looked back at Wood and Larson. "They were in a state of shock and awe with the air and artillery coming into the city. I could see it in their eyes, they were pretty scared. This was their first taste of real combat." Hanks had a different demeanor. "Mike and I were laughing and giggling like we always did."

"I can't wait to get in there," Hanks confided to Sojda. Hanks loved his job, he loved being a grunt.

With the apartments secure, Conner and the snipers wandered back to their original position on the hills. Nature called.

"I need to take a shit," said Nick Larson.

"Go for it," responded Hanks.

"No way, everybody is going to watch me and throw shit at me."

"Anytime you are around a bunch of Marines and you gotta shit, people throw rocks at you," Conner explained later. "So I yelled over, 'Hanks do you have to shit?' Hanks said, 'Yeah.'"

Hanks and Conner went down to the bottom of the hill, dug a little hole, leaned back on their hands, and relieved themselves in the Iraqi sand.

"We sat there, talking to each other and laughing. When we were done we came back on top of the hill. Larson was on one side at the bottom of the hill. Everybody was throwing rocks at him. He finished doing his business. It was a good time," Conner recalled.

After Larson finished his "business," he returned to the top of the hill and looked Hanks and Conner in the eye. "See, I told you assholes." It was all just locker room fun; everyone loved the muscular Chicago native.

Around dusk the order came down to the platoon: "We're rolling!" Directing the route to the train station and coordinating the breach into the city fell squarely on Heatherman's shoulders. The initial breach was his show. Once in the city, however, he took a hands-off approach to command, allowing his platoon commanders to lead the fight.

The platoon mounted up in Slay's tracks and made their way toward the battalion's first objective, Fallujah's train station. Lima helped coordinate the assault on the station, but the task of actually securing the objective fell largely on the Iraqi soldiers and their Marine officers and NCOs in CAP India. Lima's responsibility was to provide covering fire. Later in the battle, elements of CAP India, commanded by First Lieutenant Zach Iscol, would be integrated into 1st Platoon.

Sojda and Hank's fire team provided security for the machine gunners assigned to the platoon. Sodja said, "Mike and I got out of the tracks and went behind a berm. Our air and arty was dropping danger close. There was a lot of small arms fire. About fifteen RPGs flew over our heads. They streak by like flares and one impacted about forty meters from us."

Shortly before the train station was captured, the reporters embedded with Lima Company demanded to be returned to the safety of a rear area. While a few reporters entered the city during the battle, most preferred the safety of command posts and stayed "behind the wire," often obtaining their material from soldiers or Marines returning from the fight.

"Right before we hit the train station, the reporters bugged out. This German broad started screaming, 'This is horrible, they are bombing schools and hospitals. I have to do something.' Apparently she called someone and wanted to get out of there. I barked back, 'We don't just bomb innocent people,'" recalled Conner.

Sojda recalled the spectacle: "The journalists were petrified. I remember one guy low crawling over the back of the track, facedown.

Every so often he would poke his camera over his head and blindly take a picture without focusing in on anything. What a pussy."

The annoying task of ferrying the reporters back to a rear area fell upon Sergeant Conner. "It was a real pain in the ass. Everyone was busy, I couldn't reach the battalion commander or executive officer. We are about to attack the city. I felt like I was dealing with a piece of gear. Would someone please sign for them so I can turn them in and get back to my job? So I took them back in a track to the rear and eventually we got back into the fight."

As the platoons maneuvered into positions to support CAP India's assault on the train station, Private Sean Stokes' track suddenly broke down. "We were cramped in the tracks for hours. The next thing I know, our track breaks down. As the battalion is capturing the train station, we are ordered out of the track and told to unload everything. Lots of RPGs and small arms fire is landing near us. There's a realization you make that they are shooting at you and trying to kill you. I thought we were going to die."

When CAP India finally assaulted the station, Lima's suppressing fire proved to be lethal. According to Conner, "We lit up the train station pretty good, suppressing it. We pretty much threw everything we had at them. Tanks were blowing the hell out of it, while the tracks were hitting it with their Mark 19s and 50s." The Iraqis met minimal resistance and quickly took the station.

At approximately 0300, the platoon of combat engineers designated the "breach force" moved up to cut through a minefield and three sets of railroad tracks. Once these obstacles were passed, the engineers were to clear three lanes through a twelve-inch curb running down the center of a road perpendicular to the Marines' line of advance. The curb had to go since it would prevent even tracked vehicles from entering the city.

An accident nearly derailed Operation Al-Fajr's timeline: the smoke and dust of battle impaired a driver's vision, causing his track, carrying combat engineers, to overturn. Compounding matters, Lima mysteriously lost radio communication with the engineers blowing the breaches. Lima needed to know what was going on in a hurry.

"Someone is going to get fucking fired if we don't get comm with them right now!" barked Captain Heatherman.

"Roger that," responded Sommers. Sommers ordered one of the engineers' tracks to move back about twenty feet, and luckily communications with the engineers came back on line.

Recovering from the accident was not as easy. Heatherman knew he had to act fast. He ordered the recovery and evacuation of the engineer casualties, and quickly assembled another breach team from the detachments of assault specialists attached to his company. Coming under fire, Heatherman's newly formed engineer unit moved to the edge of the minefield.

Over the radio came the order from the engineers.

"Prepare to blow the MICLIC."

A MICLIC (M58 Mine Line Clearing Charge) is one hundred meters of rope attached to a rocket. 1,750 pounds of explosives are tied in blocks every foot or so along the rope. Each block of A3 (the solid version of C4 plastic explosive) detonates as the rocket carries the rope down range toward the target. A MICLIC will clear a path three meters wide by one hundred meters long through a minefield.

Initially, the MICLIC malfunctioned. The line charge had to be blown manually. Under muj small arms fire, one of the engineers ran out twenty-five yards into the minefield, placed a one pound block of C4 on the end of the line charge, and lit a fuse. Minutes later:

BOOM, BOOM, BOOM!

Multiple explosions drowned out the din of battle as the MICLIC detonated any enemy mines and sliced through the train tracks. However, time was running short, and thanks to the accident, the schedule of the entire operation was in jeopardy. Heatherman contacted Lieutenant Colonel Buhl.

"Sir, we can clear one or two lanes, but three isn't happening. One MICLIC is blown, we are waiting on the second. We cannot execute movement until the second MICLIC blows. What are your orders?"

"Wait till the second charge blows and send everyone through the first lane," responded Buhl.

Once the second charge blew a clear path, two mechanical monsters, "Hell Hound" and "Critter," clanked toward the city. "Hell Hound" and "Critter" were Caterpillar D9 bulldozers "up-armored" with bulletproof glass and steel plate around the driver and engine compartments. All of the dozers were reportedly shipped from Israel. On the back of one of the Israeli dozers was scrawled in Magic Marker, "To Marines, Kill them all."

Ping, Ping, Ping.

AK rounds ricocheted off the dozer's windshield.

Whoosh!

An RPG exploded on the dozer blade.

According to one of the senior NCOs in charge of the combat engineers, Staff Sergeant Steven Bodek, "When the D9s started rolling they got shot at, for a few seconds the D9s stopped, we thought someone got killed. We were worried that the bulletproof glass wouldn't work, but they took direct hits to the windshield. Over the radios we heard, 'Oh,' after a round would hit the windshield in front of their faces. After the initial shock, they kept rolling. Halfway down the breach, an RPG exploded on the D9's massive shiny silver blade. The RPG only dented the metal since the shape of the blade deflected the blast."

Staff Sergeant Bodek, who was known as "Pyro," was thirty-three years old at the time of the battle. In the States, he's a cop in Lynchburg, Virginia, and father of one boy and a girl. "I missed all their birthdays while over here." Bodek has been in the Marines and Marine Corps Reserves for the past fifteen years. Pyro carried his father-in-law's Purple Heart in the breast pocket of his camouflage blouse "My father-in-law, a retired sergeant major, is a Vietnam veteran. He never talked about the war until I was about ready to go over here. After a few drinks, he pulls this Purple Heart from his pocket that I'm holding in my hand and says, 'Now you have one, don't get another one.'"

Once in the breach, Pyro's dozers and other Marine combat engineers quickly cleared the railroad tracks and the highway curb, paving the way for the tanks.

As the entire Thundering Third sat in columns waiting for the order to attack, Bennie Conner peered across the horizon from the open hatch on his track. The sky was changing to a dark indigo blue, the signs of first light. Suddenly, tanks from 2/7, the "Ghosts," surged forward, firing their cannons and coaxial machine guns.

Sommers recalls the juggernaut that opened up on the city. "Tanks are firing away, with their main guns shooting up the city; tracks are firing their Mark 19s and .50 cals. Everything is clicking really well."

Around 0700, 3/1 surged forward. As the battalion moved toward Fallujah, the familiar sounds of battle were broken by a scene straight from the movie *Apocalypse Now*:

Da Don Da Da Don Don. Don Da Da Don Don.

The moment was electric. Many Marines got chills as Psych

Ops, their Humvees equipped with massive speakers, blared "The Flight of the Valkyries."

"I can't believe we are finally doing this. We had been talking about hitting this city since August," thought Jeff Sommers.

Ghost's penetration was largely uncontested by the enemy. As the battalion's Command Chronology reveals, "The well-concealed enemy had wisely opted against decisive battle with the heavy mechanized and armored force. Nevertheless, 2/7 thoroughly destroyed all enemy forces that did offer resistance. Additionally, 2/7 destroyed numerous obstacles and potential 'vehicles conceal-ing improvised explosive devices' along main streets. Numerous intelligence reports relayed prior to the battle indicated the pres-ence of these vehicle bombs. Many such vehicles were rendered harmless and destroyed by 2/7 Cavalry."

The Thundering Third followed in tracks and Humvees. The assault bogged down for several minutes as the massive column of vehicles, several miles long, turned into a traffic jam. Captain Heatherman and several of his NCOs dismounted and began directing the traffic. Eventually, 1st Platoon crossed the line of departure and moved into the city. Stokes recalls the moment: "When we crossed the line of departure in the tracks, .50 cals were going, tanks firing into the city, lots of stuff was blowing up—it was loud as shit. It was raining that night, it was dark and ominous, the perfect cinematography for a movie. The morning we pushed into the city. It stopped raining and the sun came out—clouds parted— it was surreal, and the calm before the storm."

7

"I'm Gonna Take You to Hell"

I'm a rolling thunder, a pouring rain
I'm comin' on like a hurricane
My lighting's flashing across the sky
You're only young but you're gonna die
—*From "Hells Bells" by AC/DC*

DAWN CAME FAST. CONNER'S "Don't Tread on Me" flag flapped gently in the breeze as 1st Platoon dismounted from their tracks. Everyone was "pumped" as 3rd Squad prepared to lead Lima Company into Fallujah. In Lima's immediate battle space, several cars were burned to a crisp, and the acrid stench of cordite lingered in the air. Omnipresent in the distance was the din of battle: screams, the chatter of small arms, and explosions. To their surprise, most of the tan-colored stone buildings remained standing.

Contrary to the battle briefing, the first rows of buildings in front of 1st Platoon were largely intact. In contrast to the battlefield preparations before the Marine battles in the Pacific, when artillery and air bombardment flattened bunkers and enemy positions, the preparatory bombardment of Fallujah was minimal.

On the strategic level, 3/1 was assigned to follow up behind the "armored battering ram" of 2/7's Abrams tanks and Bradley fighting vehicles. 2/7's job was to break through the jihadis' outer ring of defenses and disrupt their rear area. However, by itself, the armor could not perform the decisive role of engaging and displacing the enemy forces. For the muj, engaging an Abrams tank was pointless, because most of their RPGs could not penetrate the Abrams's composite armor. Most of the fighters preferred to hunker down in their bunkers and let the armored cavalry unit pass right by. While 2/7's tanks and Bradleys detonated IEDs, cut booby trap wires, prevented muj reinforcement, and killed anyone reckless enough to leave their houses, only the infantry could seize control of the real estate.

Lima Company had the difficult assignment of rooting muj fighters out of buildings using only small arms and grenades. Tanks and bulldozers, the most useful weapons for supporting infantry in urban combat, were scarce. Those under 3rd Battalion control initially went to Kilo and India, the companies assigned to lead the way on the first day of the assault. Several days would pass before Lima Company would receive tanks or D9 bulldozers to aid in clearing. In the meantime, the platoon had to rely on what they had and improvise. The force used to clear buildings rapidly escalated beyond small arms. Bangalore torpedoes and satchel charges, weapons not widely used since World War II, would prove crucial to the platoon's survival.

Lima Company faced another problem in the early stages of the battle: America's high-tech firepower, smart bombs, and artillery had largely been neutralized, in part by political pressure and in part because 3/1 did not own the battle space in front of the battalion. The battle space was occupied by 2/7, which was slicing ahead of the Marines. Dropping bombs or even mortar fire could result in friendly fire casualties.

On the first day, the battalion's mission was to penetrate about 1,500 meters into the enemy's outer defenses, clearing out the enemy fighters house by house. On day two, the plan called for 3/1 to pivot west toward the Euphrates River, smashing through the heart of the Jolan, a district boasting some of Fallujah's oldest Byzantine buildings and known for its labyrinthine alleys and streets. Lima Company would form the pivot point for the battalion's wheeling motion to the west, pushing the enemy out of the older part of the city, away from presumed civilian areas, into an "engagement area" or "kill zone."

The Jolan, the headquarters of the jihadis in Fallujah, was a defender's paradise. For months Fallujah's defenders had been converting homes into fighting positions. The bunkers were connected by a series of "mouse holes," man-sized holes knocked through walls, which allowed the enemy to move men from one area to another undetected. The concrete and stone buildings provided excellent cover and concealment, and the strong walls absorbed coalition ordnance. A typical Fallujah city block was about 100 x 200 meters long, with about one hundred stone or concrete houses. The Marines had to clear every building on the block.

Urban fighting is extremely personnel-intensive and, in terms of casualties, one of the most expensive military operations. Clearing buildings is combat at its most primitive. The fighting is up close and personal, not the pushbutton warfare that many Americans hear about and see on television. While the Marines' training and technique improved the odds, clearing was inevitably reduced to a high stakes game of Russian roulette. Kick the door in and see what's inside: either it's empty or there's a machine gun pointed at your head.

Conner's squad, reinforced by a handful of snipers and CAP India Iraqis, was the most forward element of Lima Company. Conner set the pace for Lima, and had the mission of tying into Kilo Company, which was advancing ahead of Lima. The first hour or so was surprisingly quiet. "We searched fifty houses, found massive amounts of weapons caches, RPGs, RPKs, and boxes of ammunition, but there was no sign of the enemy."

Conner was hanging with Lance Corporal Hanks's fire team, because Hanks had gone back to the tracks to get water for his men. Everyone was joking and smoking cigarettes. Conner jokingly warned Lance Corporal Nick Larson, Private First Class Jacob de la Garza, and Lance Corporal Nathan Wood: "If any one of you motherfuckers dies, I am going to kill you."

Things were too quiet," recalled Conner. Another of Conner's fire team leaders, Lance Corporal Mario Alavez, remembers getting complacent. "We were searching in the dumbest ways. We didn't see anyone. I thought maybe we'd run into a kid or a woman who was left behind. They aren't going to fuck with the Marines; they'd have to be out of their freaking minds. I thought these bitches ran just like in OIF I."

Suddenly, all hell broke loose for 2nd Platoon. Staff Sergeant Michael S. Van Daele heard "panicked" gun fire. "People are pulling the trigger as fast as they can. It's when you first see contact, or someone is shooting back at you real close." The thirty-one-year-old staff sergeant, a martial arts black belt, ordered his men forward toward the fire. One of Van Daele's ablest Marines, Sergeant William James, respected for his courage under fire and for always being at the "tip of the spear," yelled, "What happened?"

"A guy just came out of the building with a grenade in his hand, shooting an AK!" The muj fighter blew himself up with the grenade.

"Are the adjacent buildings clear?"

"No!"

Van Daele led a team in an assault on the building. "I was the first one through the door. Two guys are in the corner of the room. One has an AK in his hand. The other has an RPG. I engaged and

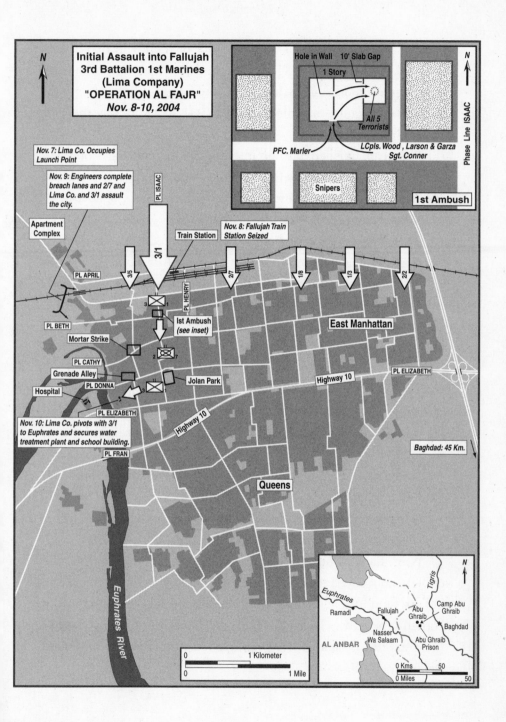

**Initial Assault into Fallujah
3rd Battalion 1st Marines
(Lima Company)
"OPERATION AL FAJR"
Nov. 8-10, 2004**

N

*Nov. 7: Lima Co. Occupies
Launch Point*

*Nov. 9: Engineers complete
breach lanes and 2/7 and
Lima Co. and 3/1 assault
the city.*

Apartment
Complex

*Nov. 8: Fallujah Train
Station Seized*

Train Station

PL ISAAC

PL APRIL

3/5 3/1 2/7 1/8 1/3 2/2

PL HENRY

PL BETH

3 ⊠ 1

1st Ambush
(see inset)

Mortar Strike

2 ⊠ 7

PL CATHY

Grenade Alley

PL DONNA

3 ⊠ 1

Jolan Park

East Manhattan

PL ELIZABETH

Highway 10

Hospital

PL ELIZABETH

*Nov. 10: Lima Co. pivots with 3/1
to Euphrates and secures water
treatment plant and school building.*

PL FRAN

Highway 10

Baghdad: 45 Km.

Queens

Euphrates River

0 — 1 Kilometer
0 — 1 Mile

Inset (top right):

Hole in Wall   10' Slab Gap

1 Story

All 5
Terrorists

PFC. Marler

LCpls. Wood , Larson & Garza
Sgt. Conner

Snipers

Phase Line ISAAC

N

1st Ambush

Inset (bottom right):

Euphrates

Tigris

Ramadi

Fallujah

Abu
Ghraib

Camp Abu
Ghraib

Baghdad

Nasser
Wa Salaam

Abu Ghraib
Prison

AL ANBAR

N

0 Kms   50
0 Miles   50

shot both of them. After I pumped a lot of rounds in them, they dropped to the floor. As I came around the corner into another room, there's another guy with an AK, and Sergeant James shot him. We moved around that room, to the next room. It was me and James. Nothing."

The team pushed farther into the house, moving along the building's interior wall. Sergeant James was standing next to the muscular Van Daele as they peered around the corner of a room.

"Make your move," Van Daele whispered to James.

Brrrrrrrrrrp! A massive amount of fire erupted from the room.

James took a step and crossed the door's threshold. As soon as his boot touched the floor, his head violently snapped backward, and his body fell right in front of Van Daele. Without hesitating, Van Daele kept pushing around the corner, shooting as fast as his finger could pull the trigger: *pop, pop, pop, pop, pop.* In one fluid motion, the muscular staff sergeant leaned down, and grabbed the back of James's flak vest with one hand, shooting with the other. "I started dragging him back as fast as I could to get him out of there. He was motionless. I didn't know it at the time, but he was hit in the left eye."

Undaunted, Corporal Butler poked his M16 into the room and fired off a burst.

"Frag out!" shouted Van Daele.

The grenade blew up the room.

Next, Lance Corporal Jose Hernandez-Soto popped around the corner and sprayed the entire room with his SAW. The grenade and bullets found their mark, leaving three dead muj slumped in the corner. One fighter had a G3 (an Iraqi knockoff of an HK assault rifle), and the others had AKs and grenades. An RPG was propped against the wall.

With the house and adjacent houses cleared of terrorists, Van Daele and his Marines tended to their fallen 2nd Platoon comrade. When they took off James's helmet, the whole back of his head was gone. According to Hernandez-Soto, "I didn't think he was dead. I pulled out a tourniquet, and started putting his brain back into his head. With tears in my eyes I yelled, 'You're still fuckin' there, you're not dead!' I really didn't think he was dead until they put him into the body bag." James had been Hernandez-Soto's fire team leader. The pair had been close friends since the company was formed.

Van Daele's men had just finished loading James's body into the truck when they heard more panic fire. First Platoon was fighting through an ambush of its own.

Conner and his squad were a few doors down the street from the building where James was ambushed, when Gunny Hackett approached Conner.

"Hey, did we clear those fuckin' houses?"

"I don't know about that house right there," responded Conner.

In fact, the house had already been swept by Corporal Bill Sojda's fire team. No one was inside when Sojda's Marines went through it, but a squad-sized element of muj had maneuvered around Conner's squad and reoccupied the house.

Conner rounded up Hanks's fire team and advanced on the building. "I kicked in the main door into what looked like some sort of an auto repair shop. I like to be up front, and I looked inside the door for a split second. A guy has a damn machine gun [RPK] pointed right at my head. He pulls the trigger and the weapon malfunctioned for some reason. It didn't shoot. So, I rolled out the way and yelled, 'Get the fuck out.' However, everything was already in motion. My Marines, being Marines, make entry into the room. Larson moved in first and caught one right in the jugular as he unloaded his magazine into the muj. As he fired, he caught one right in the juglar. Garza was the Number Two man; he was right behind Larson and grabbed him right on the handle, on the back of Larson's flak jacket. They kind of fell back into a room that was clear of the enemy. They got pinned down there."

Using standard techniques from MOUT training, Conner ordered a machine gun team led by Sergeant Jack Grantham to lay down suppressive fire on the enemy bunker. One of Grantham's men was Lance Corporal Donald Baker. Nineteen, and a resident of Victorville, California, Baker joined the Corps out of patriotism and to follow in his father's footsteps. The elder Baker was a Force Recon veteran (the Marine Corps' equivalent of Special Forces) who served three tours in Vietnam. As Baker remembered, "We got the call to move up front, fast. We stacked on the wall and were thinking, 'What's going on?' Meanwhile, rounds were hitting the wall right behind us. Sergeant Conner told us to start firing the 240 [machine gun] into the house. We busted the door into the court-yard and lay on the ground and started firing into the house. A lot of rounds were hitting near us. Sergeant Conner goes right up to the house, while Sergeant Grantham went alongside the wall, and all of a sudden rounds came right out of the wall. He made a weird turn and fell to the ground. We all thought Sergeant Grantham was hit. He got back up as fast as he could and moved towards us, but the enemy rounds destroyed his weapon. Sergeant Grantham yelled, 'Go cyclic on the house and use all the ammo you have left.' We unloaded everything we had left, which was two hundred rounds."

Conner then kicked everyone out of the courtyard and barked at Lance Corporal Michael Hanks, "Watch my ass!" The veteran NCO ran down the corridor past a room full of jihadis into the room containing Garza and Larson. "I am looking at Larson and, Jesus

Christ, there is blood all over the place, I've never seen so much blood in my life."

Conner looked twenty-year-old Private First Class Garza straight in the eyes.

"Is Larson alive?"

"I don't think so." Garza kept his composure remarkably, even after seeing his best friend killed in front of him.

Larson died in exactly the way the jihadis planned. According to Hackett, "Their discipline throughout the battle still amazes me. They just sat in the house and waited, kind of like spiders; they waited for the perfect shot, our faces or necks, since our body armor and Kevlars [helmets] protected our bodies. Their goal was to kill an American and then die."

In a bid to allow Conner and Garza to escape the house, Nathan Wood heroically charged toward the room containing the muj, spraying them with his M16 and hurling a grenade through the door. His effort to save Conner and Garza cost him his life.

As rounds from the muj in the other room ate away at the door frame above his head, Conner peeked down the corridor and saw a Marine's boots sticking out of the doorway of the room still occupied by muj fighters.

"Who the fuck is that?"

"They got Wood, they got Wood!"

"Hell no!" Conner thought to himself. He knew he had to get Garza out of the room before they were both dead.

"You go first, I am going to cover you. Just make sure someone is covering my ass!"

Conner moved into the doorway, emptied a magazine into the room filled with jihadis, and threw two grenades into the room.

"Frag out!"

Dodging a hail of bullets, Garza ran out of the room. Conner followed him into the courtyard.

Second Lieutenant Sommers was already running toward the melee when Conner reported on his radio, "We have a bunker, and are having a problem with it . . . We got a man down . . . I have two Marines killed in action . . . The guys are really stubborn, I can't get to them." Both Larson and Wood were already dead; the muj were riddling their bodies with machine gun fire.

Realizing that small arms would not suppress the bunker, Lieutenant Sommers barked over the radio: "Get a fucking rocket on it."

Four assaultmen, led by twenty-eight-year-old Chicago native Sergeant Todd "Slaughter" Rosalez, were attached to the platoon, along with several combat engineers from the 2nd Combat Engineer Battalion. The assaultmen and engineers carry rockets, handle explosives, and remove booby traps. As the battle unfolded, the engineers and assaultmen would play a pivotal role in 1st Platoon's operations.

Conner shouted an order to one of Rosalez's men, Private First Class Randell Marler, a SMAW [83mm rocket] gunner: "I want you to put a rocket in that fuckin' building."

Avoiding RPK and AK fire, Marler went to work. First, he prepped the area, making sure no "friendlies" were exposed to his rocket's back blast. Then he aimed and yelled: "ROCKET!"

The rocket hit the building at point blank range. After a massive explosion, an enormous cloud of dust billowed out of the building, and everything went quiet. The thermobaric rocket from the SMAW creates an overpressure that crushes everything it comes in contact with, while generating approximately 1,500 degrees of heat.

"Danger close" range for a SMAW rocket is fifty meters; Marler fired the rocket fifteen feet from the building. Most of the building collapsed into a heap of rubble and dust. "From all the dust and debris, we thought Marler was dead. But Marler comes trotting out of the dust, he has this walk, I call it the SMAW trot, and loads up another rocket. I was speechless," recalls Sergeant Rosalez.

Unbelievably, as 1st Platoon began the painful task of digging out the bodies of Wood and Larson, they came under fire again. According to Conner, "as we start clearing through the rubble, *pop, pop, pop,* they're still firing at us, even though they are buried under a pile of rubble."

The RPK rounds barely missed Mario Alavez.

"What the hell!"

Gunny Hackett, the senior NCO of the platoon, and the calm hand that helped guide the enlisted men of all three squads of 1st Platoon, recalled later with amazement the enemy fire coming from the rubble: "There is no way someone could live through that. Grenades, sniper fire, nearly eight hundred rounds of small arms, and a rocket were fired—I was dumbfounded they were still alive. It was the drugs, something we didn't realize until later. We started finding cocaine and adrenaline, and we started piecing it all together, that these guys were all hopped up on drugs. Like PCP users who could survive a lot of punishment." During the course of the battle, the platoon would discover many large caches of adrenaline, cocaine, and amphetamines. Spent needles littered many of the buildings the platoon cleared. According to Conner, "The terrorists just wouldn't die unless you removed their brains from their skulls."

"Put another rocket in that thing—nothing better come out alive!" barked Conner.

"It was one of the low points in my career and one of the hardest things I had to do, firing the rockets on our own dead Marines. Marler takes the shot, cool as a cat. He was so calm. He has a strut when he fires a rocket. After he fired, he would walk away almost like he was done smoking a joint," remembered Conner.

"Everyone moves up toward the house, there is no sign of life. There is no sign of life. I go up toward the house and there is moaning. I peek in the doorway, and there is a guy rolling around with a weapon in his hand, I shot him point blank in the chest. The other guy, who tried to kill me with the RPK, is buried under the rubble, weapon near his hand.

"I need someone to help me dig out the bodies," yelled Conner.

Several Marines from Conner's squad and Sergeant Kyle's 2nd Squad slowly started to uncover the bodies.

"Fuck! Fuck!" Seeing half of his fire team lying dead in the rubble, Hanks lost control. Gunny Hackett stepped forward and comforted Hanks as the men began to move the rubble off their fallen brothers.

Incredibly, the last jihadi was still alive, weapon in hand. The RPK-wielding muj still posed a serious threat to the lives of the Marines. Taking him prisoner was out of the question. The terrorist, strung out on adrenaline, was waiting to take another shot with his machine gun. Hanks spotted the muj fighter and dispatched him, allowing the men to finish clearing the rubble.

According to Kramer, "We had to pull the rubble off of them and dig them out with our shovels. Larson had been thrown back by the blast. He was under a lot of cement and rubble. We found the engagement ring he was going to give to his girlfriend, a model living in Chicago.

"After we wiped the dust off his face, Wood looked like he was sleeping. Larson and I were pretty close friends, so I didn't want to look at him too hard," recalled Kramer.

As they left the building, Lance Corporal Mike Hanks turned to Garza, the last surviving member of his fire team. All his life Michael Hanks had been a protector, the big brother. "I'm not going to let anything happen to you. I'm going to get you home alive,"

Hanks said with tears in his eyes. Garza was stunned that he survived the firefight as he tried to come to grips with the loss of his best friend, Nicholas Larson.

Second Squad Sergeant Jason Kyle recalls the emotional devastation the deaths inflicted on Conner, Hanks, and Lance Corporal Steven Wade. "After Conner and Hanks dug out Wood's and Larson's bodies, I will never forget the look on their faces. After someone dies, you always see it. The circles around the eyes get darker, a hollow look, almost like the life drained out of them—the so-called thousand-yard stare. It didn't really hit me till Wade, who had been across the street with the snipers, came over to see me. He had a tone in his voice, he knew something had happened. Wood had been his best friend."

"Hey, Sergeant Kyle, is my boy Wood alright?"

"I looked at Wade and started to choke up. I mustered all the energy I could and said, 'He is alright, Wade.' He looked at me and he knew what happened. It means a lot when you take the term brother to the max, and that's what Wade and Wood were to each other, brothers."

As Wade tearfully recalls, "When I saw Wood, tears were streaming down my face. Wood was my best friend; he was a cool dude, crazy. A white me, the white Wade."

With the assistance of the powerful Sergeant Weatherford, Conner removed the large concrete slab that had fallen on Wood. "As I kneeled down, I wiped the dust from his face, and he looked like an eighteen-year-old boy. It is one of the most haunting memories I have of this battle. After we dug out Wood and Larson, I put in a Copenhagen, took a drink of Gatorade, and carried on."

8

"Steel Rain"

We few, we happy few, we band of brothers,
For he today that sheds his blood with me
shall be my brother.
—*William Shakespeare*, Henry V

STILL STUNNED BY THE LOSS of Wood and Larson, 1st Platoon kept pushing south. Second and 3rd Squads cleared houses while 1st Squad remained in reserve, providing security for Staff Sergeant Slay's tracks.

"The death of Wood and Larson was an emotional shock. It taught us that you can't assume anything, everything has to be checked two or three times before you can call it safe; even then you have to watch your ass," recalled Jeff Sommers.

Lima Company's objective was to reach two roads inside the city designated Phase Lines Kathy and Isaac. First Platoon's objective was a school located next to a water treatment plant, unceremoniously dubbed the "tits of the Euphrates" for its large, dome-shaped filtration buildings. Resistance would prove heavier than expected, and the battalion eventually decided to "go firm," or hole up for the night, in houses near Phase Line Isaac, a road less than two thousand meters from the edge of the city.

Around midday, after a brief firefight forced the muj to melt away down the back alleys, 1st Platoon moved into a T-intersection of cobblestone streets. Realizing that a lucky RPG hit could cook everyone inside the tracks standing in the intersection, Staff Sergeant Slay snapped: "Go re-clear these houses again."

Second and 3rd Squads resumed the now all-too-familiar task of kicking in doors and clearing rooms. Conner's 3rd Squad took the left side of the road, while Sergeant Kyle's 2nd Squad went to the right. After clearing several empty houses, Hanks heard a noise.

"What the hell was that?"

Accompanied by Wade, Hanks kicked open a door and entered the building. A fighter armed with an AK appeared behind a partially open door.

"Shoot the motherfucker!" shouted Hanks.

Wade fired several rounds through the door into the man's upper body and head. A pool of blood formed around the fallen body.

Unable to see the body, Hanks asked, "Is he dead?"

Wade moved through the door. "Yeah, we got him."

Simultaneously, across the street, 2nd Squad encountered more fighters in buildings that had previously been cleared by Kilo Company. Private Sean Stokes was on point. "I was being complacent, since they said the houses were already clear. For the hell of it, I threw a flash bang grenade (they weren't very effective) into one of the rooms we were clearing. My ears were ringing so hard from all the fighting that I couldn't even hear hardly anything. So I yelled to the other guys, 'Did you even hear it go off?' They responded, 'No.' I kicked open the door and went into the room. Two guys in there stood up." Sergeant Grantham followed him in.

The muj fighters were unprepared; their weapons, AKs and an RPG, were stacked against the wall. As Stokes tried to take the men prisoner, one of the terrorists made a desperate move. According to Stokes, "The other guy stood up and grabbed the muzzle of my weapon. I threw him against the wall. He landed next to the RPG and tried to grab it. I shot him point blank in the face." Grantham and Stokes walked out of the building, and Sojda and Hanks walked in.

Despite his horrible face wound, the fighter shot by Grantham was only playing dead. "Hey, this guy is alive!" Hanks shouted as the insurgent went for an AK lying across his stomach.

Sojda quickly took action. "I could see him breathing. Grantham had put a bullet in his head, his brains were out on the floor. As he went for the AK, I grabbed his bayonet and put it right in the center of his chest and twisted it. A normal person would have died with a bullet hole in their head and multiple stab wounds, but he wouldn't die. I figured he was meant to live, so I pulled the weapons away from him and left." Drugs had given him superhuman ability to absorb punishment. Nearly all of the mujahideen 1st Platoon would encounter during the battle were high on a cocktail of drugs.

Shortly after both squads "re-cleared" the houses, a crack rang out and bullets ricocheted off the street. A sniper had opened up on 3rd Squad.

"Shit!"

One round passed so close, it burned the hair on Wade's hand. The near miss left a mark resembling a bee sting.

"You hit?" Alavez yelled back to Wade.

"No, I'm okay," responded the lance corporal, who found cover in an empty room near the street corner.

A hundred meters behind Sergeant Conner's squad, Staff Sergeant Slay's tracks, which were parked at the T-intersection, came under sniper fire. Lieutenant Sommers recalled what happened next: "The turret on his track was having problems, so he courageously got out of the track to spot and direct the fire on the sniper. We shot enough stuff there that we knocked out the sniper. As Slay was directing the fire, the enemy dropped about fifteen mortars on his position."

The mortar was one of the mujahideen's favorite weapons. With months to prepare their defenses, the terrorists had pre-targeted many positions in the city for mortar strikes. Mortar tubes concealed in underground bunkers were largely undetectable by Dragon Eyes and other airborne surveillance assets. All the mujahideen had to do was adjust their mortar tubes into the pre-marked positions and drop mortar shells into the tubes. The T-intersection had been pretargeted and was now a deathtrap—and the area was occupied by the tracks, their crewmen, 1st Squad, and many of Lima Company's support troops.

Lance Corporal Donald Baker had just finished fastening his flak vest when, all of a sudden, he heard incoming shells. "I heard the whistling and I saw the first explosion. Staff Sergeant Slay got thrown back and blood splattered on the wall behind him. I saw Grantham drop and roll behind Corporal Henning. Corporal Henning got hit by shrapnel and said, 'Ah!' Next, a piece of shrapnel hit off the side of the door and comes into the track. I saw a spark and the shrapnel hit me in the mouth. It felt like someone just socked me as hard as they could in the mouth, and I just fell over on the side of the track."

Seared in Baker's memory are Staff Sergeant Slay's last words. "Help me! Help me!"

"I am coming. I am coming!" yelled Baker.

"The mortar landed right between his feet, I got over there and he's got holes all over his body. Stuff hanging out places, blood was just pouring out of his body. His eyes are going in the back of his head and he is choking on his own blood. At that point, I realized I couldn't do anything for this guy. I watched Staff Sergeant Slay die for about thirty seconds."

Corporal Henning, a member of Baker's machine gun team, remembers thinking, "It should have been me, not him." In Henning's view, "We are Marines, we work together, live together. When you lose somebody, it's like losing a part of yourself."

Baker's attention quickly shifted to his fellow machine gunner, who was badly wounded. Despite his wound, the fellow Marine had the presence of mind to remember that security came before treating the wounded.

"Baker, come over here and help me out! I need you to post security, right quick!" screamed the wounded Marine.

"Corpsman up!" screamed Baker.

"L-16, L-33, L-37, L-41! . . ." Several "zap numbers" were called over the radio. Each Marine is assigned a zap number before the battle in case he is wounded or killed. The numbers tell the corpsmen what blood types they'll need.

Sergeant Conner's Marines weathered the mortar attack inside the house they were clearing. "We looked at each other and shook our heads. Everyone became a chain smoker as that steel rain came down."

RPGs, bullets, and mortars seemed to be exploding everywhere. In the midst of the storm of steel, Baker remembers 1st Platoon corpsman Doc Tovar braving the fire to come to the aid of the wounded Marine. "Doc Tovar rips open one of his trouser legs and there is a huge hole in his leg. Doc T patches that up and leaves." The Marine had serious shrapnel wounds all over his body. Fearing that he was going to die, Baker was yelling at him to stay awake. "I thought he was going to die. What reassured me a little bit was that he was able to go, 'Oh God, this sucks,' stuff like that. It gave me a little hope that he was going to make it."

Running as quickly as they could through the flying shrapnel, Baker and Henning carried the Marine to the medevac Humvee. On the way, they saw that almost every man in 1st Squad had been wounded.

One of the few members of 1st Squad to escape the fusillade was Lance Corporal Benjamin Bryan, who provided first aid to the wounded while laying down suppressive fire with his M16. Over the thunder of RPG explosions, Bryan started issuing orders. "Set up a casualty collection point over there," Bryan barked to several Marines.

"Vales, help Grantham." Lance Corporal Christopher Vales, acting squad medic, scurried over to Sergeant Grantham, but Grantham refused medical attention.

"Go help Taptto, he's more fucked up than me!"

Dodging mortar blasts, Vales ran to Lance Corporal, who had a large piece of razor-sharp shrapnel sticking through his throat protector into his neck. "No! No!" screamed Vales, as he swatted the Marine's hands away from the shrapnel in his throat.

"It was literally a millimeter from his carotid artery. He's sitting there pulling it out until I grabbed and pulled the shrapnel out of his throat."

Vales moved to several other wounded Marines, including the Marine who was in charge of Lima's sniper team.

"His leg was bleeding. I helped get him down and he ended up having a sucking chest wound. One of the snipers, Scott, didn't have skin from his elbow to [his] thumb, bleeding bad."

"Meanwhile," recalls Baker, "Grantham is hopping around. He doesn't have a Kevlar on, and he's walking around not knowing where everyone is at. Confused. Corporal Henning helps him find other people." Grantham refused to get medical attention for himself until he located the men in his squad.

Once the mortar shells stopped falling, the survivors and walking wounded helped move the incapacitated Marines into Humvees, where they could be transported to the battalion aid station.

Vales and Lance Corporal Giovanni Perez had to place Staff Sergeant Slay into a body bag. "Perez was having a hard time putting his body into the bag. So I grabbed him under his arms, I had his blood all over me. I was freaking out, I never saw a dead Marine before. It looked like something out of the movies. His eyes were open, mouth was open, blood was everywhere."

Gunny Hackett acknowledged that the attack was devastating. "We pretty much lost the entire squad, about twelve men, right there from the mortar attack. That was pretty heart-wrenching. I remember saying to myself, '*Okay, we are down to just two squads and it's only the first day, but we are still going to be able to do this.*'"

As the sun set on Fallujah, 1st Platoon cleared the final buildings near Phase Line Isaac. What was left of 1st Squad joined Sergeant Conner's 3rd Squad and Kyle's 2nd Squad, holed up in a stone house with a walled courtyard. Conner's men huddled on the bare stone floor, strewn with rubble and glass. It was bitter cold. Grimy blankets and quilted bedrolls, slept in by the mujahideen the night before, were scooped up and used by anyone lucky enough to find one. Everyone's nerves were on edge, and chain-smoking Marines soon filled the room with smoke. Only Bryan had any American cigarettes left. Everyone else resorted to scrounging abandoned buildings for smokes. Pine cigarettes from Korea seemed ubiquitous in the city.

A high-pitched "*Meoooooww, meoooow,*" pierced the din of battle.

"Someone shoot that fucking cat," barked a Marine.

Next, maniacal laughter and a wailing baby blared for several minutes.

"Everyone was petrified. We looked at each other and asked, 'What the hell are these guys up to?'" recalls Lance Corporal Dustin Turpen. According to Sommers, "We thought it was coming from the nearby mosque." Then the Marines heard a familiar tune:

. . . Let the bodies hit the floor
Push me again
This is the end
Skin against skin, blood and bone
You're all by yourself but you're not alone
You wanted in now you're not alone
You wanted in now you're alone
You wanted in now you're here
Driven by hate consumed by fear
Let the bodies hit the floor.

The song was "Bodies" by the rock group Drowning Pool. Now the odd noise made sense. It was not the terrorists, but a Coalition Psychological Operations team at work. The cats and babies were recordings from a movie soundtrack, and the maniacal laugh came from the movie *Predator*.

The Marines in Conner's squad spent the night talking about Wood and Larson. "Is it normal for a girl to have a seven inch clit?" roared Hanks, quoting Larson's infamous icebreaker.

"Someone recalled the night patrol where Larson landed in a pile of shit," Conner remembered later.

Hanks pulled out a CD containing songs of the Vietnam War. While the songs of Nam played in the background, barely audible over the RPGs and mortars, 1st Platoon's "go firm" house was peppered all night long by RPG rockets and small arms fire. Baker recalled, "Firefights all over the place, machine gun fire. Explosions. And I remember thinking to myself, '*Where the fuck am I?*'"

9

"Allahu Akbar"—God Is Great

When great causes are on the move in the world . . .
we learn that we are spirits, not animals, and that something is
going on in space and time and beyond space and time, which
whether we like it or not, spells duty.

—*Winston Churchill*, Rochester, New York, 1941

THE PREDAWN QUIET WAS SHATTERED BY THE ROAR OF Hanks's 203 grenade launcher, a frontline reveille of sorts. Hanks and Sojda, keeping watch, claimed they had seen shadowy figures moving in the distance.

"Get your asses up!" barked Gunny Hackett. First Platoon rose from their makeshift beds as dawn broke on November 10, 2004. As they splashed bottled water on their faces, they munched MREs and prepared for another day in the city. Lieutenant Sommers was walking around the room saying "Happy Birthday" to everybody. Most of the platoon had forgotten that November 10th was the Marine Corps' 229th birthday.

Third Battalion commander Lieutenant Colonel Willie Buhl's orders were to "drive in a linear fashion through the Jolan, push them up against the river, killing and capturing as many of the enemy as possible." The plan was to drive south, hook west toward the Euphrates River, and envelop the muj forces. Unlike November 9th, when India and Kilo took the lead, all three of 3/1's companies would be in the front line. First Platoon's objective remained the school next to the water treatment plant.

The plan required the battalion to push deeper into the section of Fallujah known as the Jolan, where hundreds of jihadis were making a stand. The Jolan, where the muj headquarters was located, is one of the oldest sections of Fallujah. Stone houses, hundreds of years old, are built on top of each other. Nearly all the houses are enclosed by courtyards and stone walls, making them miniature forts.

By November 10th, despite heavy resistance, all six main assault battalions and their attached Iraqi units had broken through Fallujah's outer defenses and pushed well over a thousand meters into the heart of the city. The muj were being overwhelmed. A jihadi cell phone call intercepted by American intelligence revealed the defenders' panic.

RX: Where is the shooting?

TX: Everywhere. In every area.

RX: What is it, artillery?

TX: Artillery, mortars, and tanks everywhere.

RX: Where are you?

TX: By the flour mill.

RX: They are attacking the flour mill?

TX: Yes, and they are attacking us too. The artillery is destroying us. All of Fallujah is in ruins. Not a house is left standing. What can stand? The tanks come down every street with artillery falling ahead of them.

RX: Get out of there!

TX: Where? How? If I go into the streets, I get shot. If I stay inside, I get shelled. And let's not forget the mortars and the aircraft and the snipers!

RX: But. . . . they said the Americans had withdrawn.

TX: The Americans are everywhere.

RX: They said Nazaal was still safe. . . .

TX: Nazaal is a war zone.

RX: Where is Arkan?

TX: No one knows.

RX: Try to make it somewhere. . . .

TX: Even if I go in the yard I will be attacked.

RX: What about Shuhada?

TX: Just bombing there, they have not entered yet.

RX: Listen, on the streets, it's just tanks right? Nobody on foot. . . .

TX: Yes, but you see, a tank is roughly as big as a house. . . . You can hit it with a rocket and it doesn't blow up.

RX: What about Jolan?

TX: War zone.

RX: They said mujahideen reinforcements were arriving.

TX: Well, they haven't arrived yet. There are still mujahideen in Askeri, only because they regrouped there from Souq and crossed over the New Road. Fallujah is finished. It is the attack of all attacks. . . .

"The attack of all attacks" was fundamentally a battle between squads. Small handfuls of men on both sides were fighting it out. Coalition air forces, artillery, and armor kept Fallujah's defenders largely, but not completely, bottled up inside the city's buildings. The terrorist squads could still move from house to house through their "mouse holes." Inside the buildings, the jihadis and terrorists, who hailed from all over the Muslim world, enjoyed the element of surprise, better cover, and sometimes even superior numbers. Doorways were turned into "fatal funnels of fire" by muj lying in ambush, pointing their weapons at the places the Marines had to enter.

Before 1st Platoon pushed west, they waited for Marine artillery to blast muj strong points. The bombardment lifted around noon. Led by Conner's 3rd Squad, the platoon advanced down a narrow east–west alley near a road labeled Phase Line Donna, driving toward the Euphrates. Initially, the Marines tried moving from rooftop to rooftop, since the ideal way to clear a house is from the top down, but this technique proved impossible to sustain since most of the roofs were several stories high.

After they cleared several empty houses, 1st Platoon encountered a large house straddling the alley directly in their path.

"How about we blast through it?" Gunny Hackett asked Sergeant Todd "Slaughter" Rosalez and Sommers.

"We have an improvised Bangalore, we can make the lane right here," responded Slaughter.

"Make it happen," ordered Sommers.

Bangalore torpedoes were last used in large numbers during the bloody Marine assaults in the Pacific. The roughly four-foot-long tubes, filled with plastic explosives, had enough punch to vaporize a large house or bunker and clear obstacles like barbed wire. Since Marine-issue Bangalores were in short supply, the combat engineers and assaultmen led by Rosalez made improvised Bangalore torpedoes by taping twenty-pound charges of C4 to two wooden engineer stakes. The charges were primed and connected with detonation cord. A non-electrical blasting cap with thirty seconds of fuse detonated the devices.*

---

*Eventually, the Marines obtained a supply of factory-made bangalores.

Carrying an improvised Bangalore, Corporal Roberts of the 2nd Combat Engineers charged the building and screamed: "Fire in the hole!" Roberts hurled the bang through an open window. A massive explosion lifted the building several feet in the air, smashing it into rubble.

After the dust settled, the platoon pushed forward. "Everyone's heads were swiveling 360 degrees looking for threats or anything out of the ordinary," recalls Slaughter. "A terrorist's bloody arm was sticking up in the rubble almost like it was reaching for the sky."

Using the Bangalore marked a turning point in the platoon's tactics. Initially, high-level fears about civilian casualties forced the Marines to clear houses by hand, employing machine guns and hand grenades. With a Bangalore, the engineers and assault-men gave Lieutenant Sommers the option of blasting a building rather than risking Marine lives to clear it. "We realized that demo [demolitions] was the way to go. Rockets and bangs go where we shouldn't," recalled Sommers. But that still left the Marines figuring out which buildings contained jihadis and which ones were empty, because they did not have permission to level every building on the block.

The platoon continued the arduous and tedious task of clearing houses. Third Squad's Lance Corporal Dustin Turpen recalls, "It would seem that the first block was always clear. They knew we were coming. And they let us think there was nobody there, and we started to get complacent. After you kick fifty doors in, and there's nobody there, it starts to become normal, that's when it always happens. It's like the fiftieth house you clear that day, and you're just trying to get it done, and that's when the shit happens."

As complacency once again threatened to set in, Lance Corporal Craig James, a survivor of the rough streets of Chicago, kicked open a door and made the platoon's first face-to-face contact with the enemy that morning. "I caught a guy, weapon in hand, chillin' in a chair and I shot him." Several other fighters tried to draw the rest of the squad farther into the house: "Mister, mister, come here." "They were trying to draw us into the room. We weren't taking the bait."

James's fire team leader, Corporal Kevin Myirski, an award-winning weightlifter, decided not to risk any more lives. "After Wood and Larson died, I was completely numb. I had no emotion. I wasn't going to risk one of my Marines going into the room," recalls Myirski. Instead, he hurled grenades into the room. However, the four muj within were safely sheltered behind the building's load-bearing wall. They continued to taunt the squad, inviting them into an ambush. "Mister, mister, come here."

Realizing grenades were ineffective, Myirski upped the ante. He called to Rosalez, who ordered Marler to fire a rocket at the outside wall of the room. The rocket blasted through the wall and killed all four jihadis.

The platoon continued its westward march through the narrow alleys. After clearing several empty houses, Lance Corporal Mario Alavez's fire team came to a house with an L-shaped entrance with two front doors, one directly in front and the other on the right side of the entrance. Which door should they use? Alavez opted to enter through the door to the left. Once inside the building, the team found a "ridiculous arsenal" containing scores of weapons, even muj versions of C4 and other munitions—and discovered that the door on the right side of the entrance was a booby trap. Two RPGs were set up on an ottoman, pointing at the doorway. If Alavez had chosen the door on the right, he and his men would have been killed.

"They survived by the grace of God," concluded Slaughter Rosalez.

As Rosalez was planting C4 to blow the weapons cache, somebody made a noise.

"I just heard something," Wade nervously reported.

"The house has been cleared," Rosalez shot back.

A shadow appeared on the stairs and seemed to move.

"Blast it," barked Rosalez to Wade.

The apparition bolted upstairs. Rosalez ordered Wade and everyone inside to leave the building. "Then I ordered a corporal of the engineers we nicknamed "the Jack Rabbit" to throw his second field-expedient Bangalore into the house. Jack Rabbit yelled, 'Fire in the hole!' The front of the house collapsed and all of the rounds inside the house started going off." Several jihadis tried to break out windows from the second floor but were burned alive by the fire erupting from the Bangalore.

The platoon advanced to an intersection and bounded across the street into a narrow alley. It was midafternoon and Sommers's Marines were running out of time, thanks to the delays caused by the artillery prep in the morning and the frequent resistance. They were in danger of failing to reach their objective, the school next to the water treatment plant, on time. To speed up the advance, Sommers directed the attached CAP India Iraqi soldiers to handle the clearing while 1st Platoon pushed down the narrow alley toward the school.

The quiet was shattered by the blast of a grenade. Sommers recalled, "Third Platoon is in a house near us. I thought they threw the grenade. So I yelled 'Hey motherfuckers! There's friendlies over here!' Gunny Hackett looks at me and says 'I don't think that's a friendly grenade.' Then jihadis start screaming 'Allahu Akbar! Allahu Akbar!' We're like, 'Oh.'" Private Stokes yelled back, "*Inte manyook! Inte manyook!*" (You are a man who enjoys sodomy).

Sommers began to ready 3rd Squad and CAP India for an assault on the building, but they were driven back up the alley by a flurry of grenades. Peterson covered the retreat by blasting the building with his SAW (squad automatic weapon).

Grenades continued to chase the Marines up the alley.

"Grenade! Grenade!"

"Hurry up!" yelled Stokes. The young Marine ran unharmed past a ball-shaped British Mills grenade just as it detonated, but he couldn't outrun all the enemy projectiles. Another grenade landed between the twenty-year-old private and the platoon radio operator, Lance Corporal Bradley Adams.

"It picked him up off the ground about six feet and blew the radio off his back," recalls Stokes. "I felt about six pieces of the grenade hit me. It burned really bad. As I turned around, Adams hit the ground. I thought he was dead. He's my friend. I was so pissed that I started firing into the doorway where they seemed they were coming from."

Running up the alley behind Stokes and Adams was Stokes's fire team leader, Lance Corporal Heath Kramer. "All of a sudden, I hear a fuckin' boom! And my foot went numb. And I'm like, 'What the fuck was that?' And I looked down to see if my foot was still attached to my leg, and someone yells, 'GRENADE!'

"The insurgents were right behind me. I threw a grenade back at them. I don't think I hit anybody. At the time, everything was so loud, I didn't even hear them yell "GRENADE!" I just had a tunnel vision and kept running back toward the house where I linked up with Gunny."

In the house, Corporal Abudayeh said to Kramer, "I don't know how you're still standing." Abudayeh had seen the grenade detonate next to Kramer's foot—but only the blasting cap had exploded, not the grenade itself. "I prayed every day," said Kramer. "I was really thankful when I got back to the house. I don't know if it was just the blasting cap that blew up, but whatever it is, I'm just glad to be alive." Miraculously, no one was killed by the hailstorm of grenades, but eight men were wounded from shrapnel.

In an attempt to eliminate the jihadis throwing the grenades, Marler leveled his SMAW at the building. "ROCKET!" The rocket skipped across the wall, and set ablaze a nearby grove of palm trees.

"Did we get 'em?" barked Conner. The crackle of jihadi gunfire answered the squad leader's question. "I don't have the geometry!" Marler responded coolly. Because Marler could not get a rocket on the target, a squad of CAP India troops led by Sergeant Alvarado prepared to assault the building. Third Squad moved up to support Alvarado's assault. Conner's team leader, Mario Alavez, recalled pushing along a wall toward the target building and nearly being hit. "The rounds whizzed right by my hand and burned the hairs on my skin. Even though they miss, it hurts like hell."

Then it was Sergeant Conner's turn to receive another miraculous reprieve from death. "Sergeant Conner was right behind me. A machine gun opened up again, Conner stepped back to get a better shot on him, and machine gun rounds completely outlined where his head had been a second earlier. They just went around where his head was and hit the wall behind him, like the scene from the movie *Pulp Fiction*," recalls Alavez. Undeterred by the small arms fire, Sergeant Alvarado's Iraqi troops launched their assault. "One of the [CAP India] guys picked up his AK, stood straight up right near where Conner was standing, exposing himself, and went full auto on the building. I stopped shooting just to look at him, this MF was so badass," said Alavez.

The soldier, nicknamed Omar, was a former Iraqi special forces soldier in Saddam's army. He continued to expose himself to fire as the CAP India troops pushed forward. After the battle of Fallujah,

Omar would be betrayed by another member of CAP India. While driving to an assignment with the Army, his car was riddled by machine gun bullets.

In the fusillade of RPK and AK fire, a bullet pierced Sergeant Alvarado's thigh. Blood was everywhere.

"Corpsman up! Corpsman up!"

"And that's when Hanks and I go chargin' in there, and got down behind this log, and we found this crispy critter—a body that apparently got hit by Marler's rocket that just got cooked," recalled Conner. "We were still taking shots. We couldn't see where the hell they're coming from. All of a sudden, an insurgent came down the stairs and Hanks shot him. His body came rollin' down the stairs."

"Open the door! Open the door and I'm gonna carry him out!" screamed Hanks. Fearlessly, the twenty-two-year-old lance corporal threw Alvarado over his shoulders in a fireman's carry, kicked in the door, and carried the wounded Marine through the AK fire to safety. As Heath Kramer watched Hanks rescue Alvarado, he was thinking, *"Hanks isn't a garrison Marine, but he is flawless on the battlefield."*

The beefy lance corporal carried the wounded Marine about one hundred meters to the platoon's corpsman, leaving Alvarado to be medevaced. Braving more fire from the house, he returned to Conner's position behind the log. Exhausted, Hanks looked at Conner and asked: "Dude, should we clear this house?"

As Conner and Hanks prepared to charge the jihadis on the second floor, they were unaware that they were about to be attacked from the rear. A muj barreled down a set of stairs behind them and aimed his AK at Hanks and Conner. In the nick of time, a burst of fire hit him squarely in the face. He tumbled down the stairs and landed near Hanks.

"Lance Corporal Hanks, I got him," shouted Private First Class Jacob de la Garza. With a large grin on his face, Conner turned to de la Garza. "Hey, welcome to the club."

"Later we had a little party for Garza that night. If it wasn't for Garza, Hanks and I might have been smoked right then and there; we wouldn't be alive," recalled Conner. For the fourth time that day, 1st Platoon men had been miraculously spared.

About an hour after surviving "Grenade Alley," the platoon reached its objective. As the Marines prepared to storm the school, a lone gunman opened up on them from a balcony, only to be dispatched by assaultman Lance Corporal Peter Suguitan's well-aimed SMAW rocket.

Seconds later, the roar of incoming friendly artillery drowned out the din of small arms fire. Marine 155 rounds started landing "danger close," fewer than one hundred meters from the platoon. Several rounds landed fifty meters from the platoon, so close that the men should have been vaporized. *"God, I hope that's ours,"* thought Sojda.

Apparently, one of 3/1's other companies had spotted jihadis heading toward the Euphrates and called in the artillery strike. Luckily, 1st Platoon found an open door and took shelter from the incoming arty rounds inside the schoolhouse.

The school contained large weapons caches, but it was empty of fighters. Minutes earlier, however, the building had been packed with jihadis. "We found several water bottles with the froth still on the rims of the bottles and half-eaten food that was still warm," recalled Rosalez.

First Platoon went firm for the night in the schoolhouse, secure in the knowledge that their mission was accomplished and they would be withdrawn from combat the next day. In the rubble-strewn rooms, the men "rat fucked" several boxes of MREs (Meals

Ready-to-Eat), picking out the cookies, candy, and other goodies; swilled down Frost-flavored Gatorade; and chain smoked like fiends. Nearly everyone in the platoon smoked cigarettes to ease the strain of battle. Hanks pulled out a tiny set of speakers and a CD he brought specially for the battle, containing "Wooly Bully" and "Pale Shade of White," and played the Vietnam-era tunes for the squad.

The music was interrupted by an explosion near the building.

"Fuck!"

"That was close."

A massive controlled detonation—at least that's what most of the men thought it was—blew out the window of the room where 3rd Squad was sleeping. RPGs rocked the side of the house, followed by the usual staccato small arms fire. Nearly every night in Fallujah, the enemy peppered the platoon's "go firm" house with RPGs and small arms. Psyops paid a visit to the area, and the men soon heard the familiar *Predator* laugh and wailing of cats. During the night, scores of muj re-infiltrated sections of "cleared" city, while the main body of the jihadists slipped farther south. Before Private Stokes went to sleep, he remembered "getting down and praying, thanking God I survived another day."

10

Back into the Fray

I hope this is the dark part of the night,
which is generally just before day.
—*General Nathanael Greene*

IN THE EARLY MORNING HOURS OF NOVEMBER 11, THE MEN
woke up to a flurry of activity. Gunny Hackett barked, "Move out!
You have fifteen minutes to pack your shit and get into the tracks!
We gotta leave right now!" The scene was chaotic, but remarkably,
1st Platoon got all their gear stowed and men on board the tracks in
less than half-an-hour.

"Hey, are we moving north?"

"We're going south."

"Shit!"

Cold reality sank in. Instead of moving north, out of the battle
and back to Camp Abu Ghraib, as the original command briefing
called for, 3/1 was pushing deeper into Fallujah. "It was a bad feeling knowing you're going into Fallujah," recalled Mario Alavez. "It
was even worse knowing you're going further into Jolan toward
Queens. Now that was a bad fucking feeling." Heath Kramer
remembers thinking, "Oh man, another day, so many of our guys are

down, when's it my day?" Throughout Fallujah, the other allied battalions faced stiff resistance as they pushed south into the heart of the city.

At approximately 10:00 a.m., 1st Platoon was approaching Iraqi Highway 10, dubbed Phase Line Fran. Fran, the east–west highway that bisects Fallujah on its way to Baghdad, was an important milestone. Once Fran was taken, most of the jihadists' organized defensive rings inside the city would be breached. The men in the platoon, however, weren't thinking about the strategic situation. For them, it was just another day of trying to stay alive.

First Platoon dismounted from the tracks and resumed the deadly business of clearing hundreds of houses and buildings. As soon as the platoon pushed forward, a black-clad fighter wearing tennis shoes dashed across the street.

"Hey, there's a motherfucker!"

"Got him."

The jihadi was cut down by Private First Class Jackie Damico's SAW. Everyone's adrenaline was pumping. Sweat was pouring down their faces as they baked under the Iraqi sun.

Conner's 3rd Squad took the lead as the platoon pushed forward. The men passed a car loaded with weapons and explosives. *"There's probably lots of muj running around here,"* Conner thought to himself.

At the end of an alley, Conner's men found themselves standing in front of the largest building they had seen in Fallujah, a massive twin-towered apartment complex with shops on the first floor. Conner directed his fire teams to split up and start clearing. The men swept through a gun shop and cleared the lower levels. After making his way to the top of the first tower, Conner looked across the smoking ruins of Fallujah, thinking, *"What an awesome view of the city."*

Third Squad and 2nd Squad entered a door on the first floor and started clearing the second tower.

As Conner's men methodically cleared each room, they found al-Qaeda propaganda lying everywhere. The men didn't realize it right away, but they had stumbled upon one of al-Qaeda's head-quarters in Fallujah. The recently occupied building had been hastily abandoned by the terrorists.

Conner was the first man into the room that held the jackpot—al-Qaeda's computer lab. The room, strewn with broken chairs, monitors, and keyboards, still contained a dozen networked computers. The PCs turned out to be an intelligence treasure trove. Marine Intelligence teams would glean priceless information about the operations of al-Qaeda's commander in Iraq, Abu Musab al-Zarqawi.

Hanks's fire team found large caches of adrenaline, along with syringes. Other rooms contained bomb-making materials, such as coils of copper wire and bags of black powder.

Lima Company's heavy weapons platoon, led by First Lieu-tenant Carin Calvin and Staff Sergeant Josh Adamson, made a grisly discovery.

"Hey, look down these stairs." Using the surefire flashlight on the bottom of his M16, Adamson probed the darkness. "My God, there were bloody handprints and claw marks all over the walls. The sand floor was soaked with dried blood. A metal torture device or rack to stretch people out was propped against the wall," he recalled.

After notifying the Lima Company HET (Human Intelligence Exploitation Team) about al-Qaeda's torture chamber and comput-ers, the heavy weapons platoon scrambled up several flights of stairs to the roof, where they set up a mortar fire support base. Third Squad was also deployed on the roof.

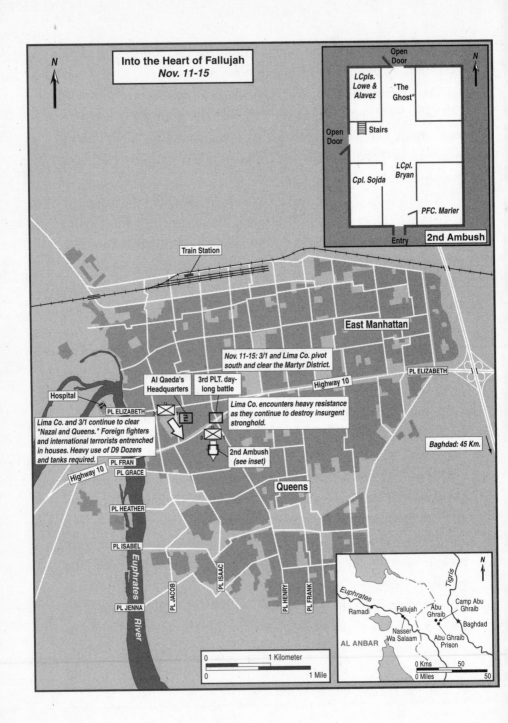

Into the Heart of Fallujah
Nov. 11-15

2nd Ambush

LCpls. Lowe & Alavez

"The Ghost"

Open Door

Open Door

Stairs

Cpl. Sojda

LCpl. Bryan

PFC. Marler

Entry

Train Station

East Manhattan

Nov. 11-15: 3/1 and Lima Co. pivot south and clear the Martyr District.

Hospital

Al Qaeda's Headquarters

3rd PLT. day-long battle

PL ELIZABETH

Highway 10

PL ELIZABETH

Lima Co. encounters heavy resistance as they continue to destroy insurgent stronghold.

Lima Co. and 3/1 continue to clear "Nazal and Queens." Foreign fighters and international terrorists entrenched in houses. Heavy use of D9 Dozers and tanks required.

Baghdad: 45 Km.

2nd Ambush (see inset)

PL FRAN

PL GRACE

Highway 10

Queens

PL HEATHER

PL ISABEL

PL JACOB

PL ISAAC

PL HENRY

PL FRANK

Euphrates River

PL JENNA

0   1 Kilometer

0   1 Mile

Euphrates

Tigris

Ramadi

Fallujah

Abu Ghraib

Camp Abu Ghraib

Baghdad

Nasser Wa Salaam

Abu Ghraib Prison

AL ANBAR

0 Kms   50

0 Miles   50

Almost immediately after both squads had established their positions, the rooftop started taking fire. Third Squad was ordered to reply with their 203s against targets to the south. Alavez and Hanks went to work on a series of windows, thought to be occupied by muj fighters.

Disregarding his own safety, Lieutenant Calvin stood up on the roof and started directing fire on muj positions. "Put one here! Put a 203 over there!" "He looked like a freaking pirate waving his hat in the air," recalled Alavez.

Calvin was busy spotting enemy positions when an AK round ripped through his flak vest. "They said it was luck, a quarter-of-an-inch and I would have been in a wheelchair. It came in through my flak vest and went along my back, underlining my Marine tattoo, ricocheted off my plate, and came out the other side of my flak vest. It was a tracer, so it actually cauterized the entire wound." Calvin refused evacuation and continued to call fire down on muj strong points.

From their rooftop vantage point, Conner and Calvin spotted scores of mujahideen pouring out of a large mosque to envelop 3rd Platoon. The Marines had run into a hornet's nest—one of the largest and most heavily defended bunker complexes in Fallujah.

"Veteran's Day 2004 was the day that wouldn't end for us," recalled 3rd Platoon's Sergeant Dan Tremore, a twenty-five-year-old Wisconsin native. About an hour before the ambush, Tremore's men had discovered a children's ice cream truck loaded with a massive arsenal of weapons. "It wasn't ice cream inside, there were thirty RPGs, brand new Dragunov sniper rifles, mines, grenades, everything." The "Trojan horse" ice cream truck exemplified the willingness of the jihadis to go to extreme lengths to exploit the American rules of engagement. Fallujah's defenders used mosques and schools as fighting positions. Hospitals became weapons caches, and ambulances were used to transport troops and supplies to the battlefield. Despite their religious protestations, nothing was sacred to Fallujah's defenders.

Third Platoon started clearing buildings just one block from Phase Line Fran. Minutes later, a sniper pinned down Tremore's squad. After locating the sniper, the Marines literally burned him out by turning a parked car in front of his building into a flaming Molotov cocktail. Burning fuel from the car's gas tank engulfed the building, killing the sniper.

With the sniper out of the way, Tremore's squad and the rest of of 3rd Platoon moved forward, unwittingly pushing into the jaws of the ambush. When muj fighters streamed out of the nearby mosque to flank 3rd Platoon's position, Tremore's squad ducked into a wrecked, multistory building, later dubbed "The Alamo." A torrent of small arms fire engulfed the Marines as they entered the building. The fire was so heavy, Tremore's men resorted to using mirrors to look around corners for gunmen.

"They were like ants moving around everywhere. We fired upon them with our 203s and small arms and hit three or four of them, including one who took a nosedive off a building after he was hit. We kept firing on them until we ran out of 203 rounds," recalled Tremore. Third Platoon's position became more precarious as Corporal Theodore Bowling's fire team moved onto another rooftop to gain a better field of fire. Bowling was immediately pinned down by muj fire.

"I got them all over me!" Bowling screamed over the radio. Pictures from a Dragon Eye UAV revealed that 100 to 150 fighters had surrounded 3rd Platoon's position.

Lance Corporal Michael Hebert, a member of Bowling's fire team, recalled the action. "There was no way we could pop our heads up. We had holes in our helmet covers. We had to use mirrors on sticks to aim and we held our weapons above our heads and pulled the triggers."

Meanwhile, Calvin's and Conner's men were continuing to provide fire support from atop the tower. As the melee heated up, Calvin devised a fire plan of air, artillery, and mortars to relieve pressure on Bowling's squad. However, air support was not immediately available, as all assets were conducting other missions.

"Everyone just opened up, SAW gunners, everybody. They were just burning through magazines," recalled Tremore. Bowling's M16 ran out of ammo, so he switched to an AK he had picked up from a dead jihadi.

An AK round struck Bowling in the neck, shattering a vertebra. Lance Corporal Ralph Arzate, another fire team leader, was loading a 40mm high-explosive grenade into his M-203 grenade launcher when Bowling was hit. Azarte heard a spectral voice say, "Oh, I'm hit." Later, Azarte insisted "It was not [Bowling] talking. He had lost the air in his neck." A final bullet pierced the Marine's head, taking his life.

"I didn't know how bad his wounds were, so I was pulling him out. His skin turned pale yellow. Then I got hit," recalled Azarte. Crippled by the loss of two fire team leaders, the squad kept on fighting anyway.

Third Platoon was rapidly getting desperate. "We need air now!" 3rd Platoon's CO screamed over the radio to 3/1's air officer.

"We are still working on it," responded the officer. The man was doing his best. There simply weren't enough planes in the air to cover all the hot spots in Fallujah. Every plane was already booked on other critical missions, supporting soldiers and Marines who were pinned down elsewhere in the city.

"We were up there on our own. Trying to pull the wounded off. We had about eight wounded and one killed. We were taking RPG fire and getting hit real hard. We were just firing at a cyclic rate. We just kept firing. They were all over the place. Some ran into the street and were just getting chopped down," recalled Tremore.

"Out of ammo!" Magazines were flying everywhere as the Marines burned out their weapons, holding off the jihadis trying to overrun 3rd Platoon's position. Some of the men charging up the stairs to rescue Bowling were knocked back down the stairs by an exploding RPG round. "Corporal West got his second Purple Heart in the leg but kept running up there. Eventually, they got to Corporal Bowling; Doc Coker put a trake in him and tried to bring him back, but couldn't do it. They just dragged him off the rooftop as we all fell back. An Iraqi, Sammy, he would never leave our side. He was one of the last men to leave the building," recalled Tremore.

Meanwhile, artillery and mortar fire, directed by Lieutenant Calvin, rained down around the beleaguered platoon. The mujahideen were within fifty meters of the Marines. At that distance, the indirect fire falling on the muj was considered "danger close," but the Marines had to risk being hit by their own artillery or they would be overrun by the muj. The first arty round fell short, hitting the building sheltering Bowling's squad. Fortunately, no Marines were wounded by the friendly fire. The firefight had been going on all day when Marine jets finally arrived, making several drops on the muj positions surrounding the platoon. Tanks arrived and destroyed the bunker complex while engineers blew up the infamous ice cream truck. Bowling's squad alone was credited with killing thirty mujahideen before they were able to extract themselves and their fallen comrade's body from the Alamo.

Reflecting on the firefight, Hebert said, "That was the most significant day in my life. I can remember the smell of burning rubber

and gun powder. The air was so thick it was hard to breathe sometimes. I don't think anybody was afraid to die, but this shit was
scary."

As 3rd Platoon battled in the Alamo, 1st Platoon resumed its
drive south. That morning, several 1st Squad men injured in the
November 9 mortar attack had returned to duty. First Squad was
reconstituted and back in business.

One of the first houses 1st Platoon cleared contained a nasty
surprise. Stokes kicked in a door and found wires leading into several black boxes. One of the assault specialists, Lance Corporal
Suguitan, quickly determined they were not the typical booby traps
designed to take out a man or two. Instead, the entire building was
set to blow, destroying any squad attempting to clear it. The building itself was an IED.

They didn't take any chances. Suguitan and Rosalez reported
the situation to Gunny Hackett.

"Hey Gunny, this entire building is wired."

"Pull everyone back, we're going to blow it."

As the platoon withdrew, Suguitan prepped a satchel charge.
Commonly used in World War II, a satchel charge is a bag containing approximately twenty pounds of plastic explosives with a thirty-
second fuse. Like Bangalores, they are devastating tools for rooting
defenders out of bunkers.

"Fire in the hole!" screamed Suguitan.

BOOM! The satchel charge practically cut the building in half.
The building creaked and teetered, but it didn't fall.

"Do you wanna clear this house?" Gunny Hackett asked Rosalez.

"No one could have lived through that," Rosalez responded.
"Whoever's in there is dead."

"Its funny, we might actually get of this day alive," murmured a
relieved Lance Corporal Benjamin Bryan.

"Keep your hopes up," replied Private First Class Eduardo Vaquerano.

The men failed to take into account the effect of muj drugs. Hearing footsteps coming from the shattered house, they assumed other members of the platoon had entered the building. Suddenly, two dusty, black-clad jihadis, hyped up on adrenaline, emerged from the rubble to engage the Marines. The men were bleeding from the eyeballs, but they managed to get a few rounds off before Hackett killed both of them with his M4, a shortened version of the M16.

Another muj wearing an explosive vest was attempting to escape through a mouse hole when he ran into Bryan and Vaquerano. "His face was filled with surprise when he saw us. I think he knew he was about to die," recalled Vaquerano.

The jihadist lunged at Vaquerano.

"Shoot him!" yelled Bryan to Vaquerano.

"Shoot him!"

Vaquerano remained motionless. Bryan shot the man twice in the stomach.

Bryan shot him five more times.

"Fuck!"

"Fuck!"

The drug-crazed muj kept on coming. "As he reached up with his bloody arm and tried to choke us, Bryan put a ten-round burst into him," recalled Vaquerano.

Even after putting seventeen rounds into the muj's body, Bryan still had to shoot him in the head to prevent him from detonating his vest. As the muj's eyes rolled back and he finally expired, Bryan crouched down and put out his middle finger. "Fuck you!"

Stunned, Gunny Hackett turned to Bryan and Rosalez. "How the hell did they survive?"

3rd Squad, November 13, 2004. Standing, from left to right: Connor, Alavez, Turpen, Hanks, Sojda. Kneeling, from left to right: Garza, Contreras, Wade, Lowe. Group pictures later became taboo because every time a photo was taken, a member of the platoon was soon killed. (*Author photo*)

Michael Hanks, November 17, 2004. (*Author photo*)

Above left: Corporal Bill Sojda; Hanks' "best friend in the world." **Above right:** Sergeant Conner, after Chechen ambush, November 17. (*Author photos*)

Below left: Best friends: Larson and Garza. The two were inseparable and often hard to tell apart, hence the nickname "Garson." **Below right:** Nathan Wood. (*Photos courtesy of R. Wood*)

USMC Corporal Adel Abudayeh dressed
as an Iraqi during a "Trojan Horse"
operation mounted by Lima Company
to gather intelligence outside Fallujah.
(*Author photo*)

Michael Hanks and Benjamin Bryan
(*Photo courtesy of J. Sommers*)

Michael Hanks goofing
around with a fellow Marine.
(*Photo courtesy of R. Wood*)

Derick Lowe in "prison." First Platoon was billeted in empty cells in Iraq's infamous Abu Ghraib Prison. *(Photo courtesy of J. Sommers)*

Sgt. Todd "Slaughter" Rosalez who led 1st Platoon's contingent of Marine Assualtmen. Assualtmen and combat engineers blow up buildings by employing rockets, satchel charges and Bangalore torpedoes—the same explosives used sixty years earlier on the beaches of Normandy and Iwo Jima. Assualtmen and Combat Engineers were some of the bravest men on the battlefield since they had the thankless task of disarming IEDs, booby traps and detonating captured Jihadi "suicide vests." *(Author Photo)*

Steven Wade, best friends with Nathan Wood. *(Photo courtesy of D. Turpen)*

Michael Hanks with Iraqi children. *(Photo courtesy of J. Sommers)*

Platoon leader Lt. Jeffrey Sommers (left) and Gunnery Sergeant Matthew Hackett (right). *(Author photo)*

Private Sean Stokes carries his weapon and a fallen buddy's weapon home. Stokes single-handedly killed nine terrorists in Fallujah. (*Author photo*)

Author in Fallujah, having survived a second ambush, November 18. (*Author photo*)

"The funniest man" in 1st Platoon, Lance Corporal Terry James. (*Author photo*)

1st Platoon's machine gunners (left to right) Henning and Baker. (*Author photo*)

During the battle nearly all the fighters encountered by Lima Company were high on various drugs, such as cocaine and adrenaline. The drugs allowed them to absorb enormous amounts of damage to their bodies. The terrorists fought to the death even after being buried alive in the rubble of collapsed buildings. (*Author photo*)

"Fire in the Hole!" 1st Platoon clears a building full of insurgents. The Marine with the long tube is using a Bangalore torpedo, an explosive device widely used on Normandy's Omaha Beach. (*Author photo*)

"Pathway to Death."
A fighter killed by
Lima Company.
(*Author photo*)

First Platoon advancing on enemy positions. *(Author photo)*

A battle-scarred mosque minaret used by the Muj as a sniper's nest. Over half of Fallujah's mosques were used as fighting positions or weapons caches by Fallujah's defenders. Once they were used for military purposes they became legitimate military targets. *(Author photo)*

"Natasha," an Israeli D-9 armored bulldozer on loan to Lima Company. By the end of the battle, D-9s were being used to demolish enemy defenses, because the terrorists were fighting like the Japanese in WWII—to the death. (*Author photo*)

Lima's attached combat engineers. Staff Sergeant Steven Bodek gives the "thumbs up." Stripped of modern technology, 1st Platoon was forced to fight like its WWII forebears. The platoon may not have survived the battle had it not been for the engineer's intrepid service. (*Photo courtesy of S. Bodek*)

Laser-guided bomb destroys enemy positions several hundred meters in front of 1st Platoon's position. (*Author photo*)

Most of the men suffered shrapnel wounds from enemy grenades or mortars. Many members of 1st Platoon concealed their wounds so they could continue to fight, rather than leave their Marine brothers in the middle of a battle. Nearly the entire platoon received the Purple Heart; some men received two. (*Photo courtesy of J. Sommers*)

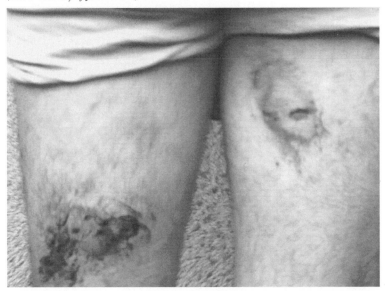

A typical weapons cache found by 1st Platoon. Fallujah's defenders pre-positioned weapons throughout the city so they could drop their weapons and fall back unmolested to alternative positions. The U.S. rules of engagement forbade firing on unarmed people. (*Photo courtesy of C. Vales*)

Lt. Calvin's bullet scarred back. The bullet barely missed his spine and heart by an inch. The round underscored his Marine tatoo. (*Photo courtesy of W. Buhl*)

Staff Sergeant Steven "Pyro" Bodek shows the author a Mujahedeen face mask worn by a man he had killed two days earlier. (*Photo courtesy of Gunnery Sergeant David Wilson*)

A seemingly innocuous-looking children's ice cream truck was used as a traveling arsenal by the terrorists. *(Photo courtesy of Gunnery Sergeant David Wilson)*

Below left: "Terrorist treats." The interior of the ice cream truck. *(Photo courtesy of Gunnery Sergeant David Wilson)* **Below right:** Members of 1st Platoon push forward into a section of the city called "Queens," an Al Qaeda stronghold. The body of a recently killed foreign fighter is sprawled out in the foreground, lying beside a live grenade he tried to hurl before he was cut down. Another fighter located near him was wearing a suicide vest (ammunition chest harness filled with plastic explosives). *(Author photo)*

Sgt. Conner, reflecting and experiencing a sense of foreboding, November 17th. (*Author photo*)

Author's bloodsoaked boots, stained while carrying a fallen Marine from the Chechen ambush. (*Author photo*)

Gunny Hackett after ambush on November 17th. (*Author photo*)

Ambush on Nov. 18th.
A mortally wounded
Iraqi soldier is treated by
Lima Company's corpsmen.
(Author photo)

Sgt. Conner after the
Chechen ambush
on November 17th.
Conner took three bullets
in his arm. *(Author photo)*

Ceremony honoring Lima's fallen.
(Author photo)

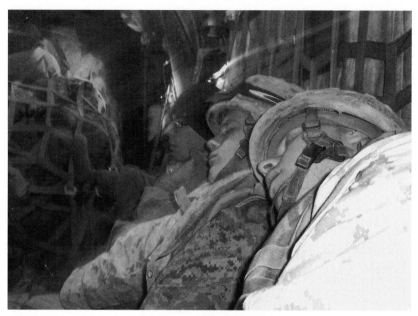

Brothers in arms on their way home from the battle of Fallujah. Most of the Marines would return to Iraq seven months later for their third tour of duty. The unit was sent to Haditha, the small town near the Syrian border that became infamous following allegations that Marines murdered innocent civilians. *(Author photo)*

Most members of 1st Platoon stenciled the names of their fallen brothers on their helmets. *(Author photo)*

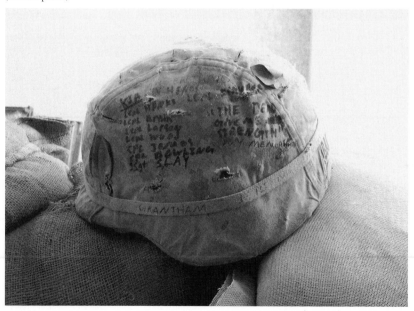

"There's no way anyone should have lived through that. No way. Drugs again," replied Slaughter.

First Squad soon came to another house suspected to contain the enemy.

The Marines stacked against the wall of the house, and Lance Corporal Vales prepped a grenade.

"Frag out!"

The grenade hit the banister near the house's front door, rolled back toward 1st Squad's stack, and detonated. Five Marines, including the squad's acting leader, Sergeant Shawn Pourier, were wounded and had to be medevaced. The incident earned Vales the nickname "Ted," a reference to the Unabomber, Ted Kaczynski.

Scant hours after being reconstituted, 1st Squad had again ceased to exist as a combat unit. The survivors were divided between Conner's and Kyle's squads. "I wanna roll with Conner," Bryan told Sommers.

Wiping sweat off his face and taking a swig from a water bottle, Bennie Conner was studying a small, tan-colored house. It looked similar to most of the houses in Fallujah, but something seemed fishy. By now many of the men in the platoon were acquiring a sixth sense about when terrorists were lurking behind doors. Most of the squad was stacked outside the house.

"I think I heard a noise," murmured Alavez. Bryan, now part of Conner's squad, kicked in the door, but only the top half of the door caved in.

"Prep a grenade," barked Sojda to Alavez. "I gave him the grenade and thought, '*Shit, he's going to get my kill*,'" Alavez recalled.

"Frag out!" The explosion spread dust and smoke everywhere, as Conner rushed through the door.

A ghost-like muj emerged from the cloud of dust. "Conner puts one right through this guy's forehead. Blood spatters against the wall and bone is sticking out of his skull," recalled Alavez. Two more muj ran down the steps and were cut down by a burst from Conner's M16. After clearing the building, Conner and most of his squad emerged to meet Gunny Hackett on the street. Conner smirked at Hackett and swaggered down the street like John Wayne.

"Bad guys 0, good guys 3."

It was kill or be killed. After so many close calls, and the deaths of two men, Conner's squad was in the mood for revenge. Hanks, in particular, wanted to avenge the deaths of Larson and Wood, the men from his fire team who had been killed. By this time, the men had discovered that after killing once, it becomes easier to kill again.

Hanks countered the deadliness of combat with humor, but for many Marines, life and death boiled down to fate. "When it is your time to die, it is your time, and there is nothing you can do about it." A number of the men adopted a different approach. For some men, it's easier to cope if they consider themselves already dead.

Moving south near Phase Line Fran, the platoon witnessed several of the macabre scenes that only come with war. With a SMAW rocket, Marler destroyed a house containing several mujahideen. All that remained of one man was the lower half of his body kneeling on the ground, with his exposed buttocks in the air. The Marines dubbed him "Assman."

Feral cats and dogs were roaming the streets, providing a surreal backdrop to the battle. All the former pets were starving to death; their only source of food was the rotting bodies of the dead. The fighting was still too intense for the coalition's Graves Registration units to clean up the dead muj bodies. As Conner's group cleared a house near Phase Line Fran, they saw a hungry white cat emerge from the body of a headless corpse. "Catman," someone murmured.

The final house in their sector was occupied by several muj, whom they dispatched with rockets and grenades. The day was drawing to a close, and 1st Platoon needed to find a "go firm" house, preferably a stone house with a walled courtyard that could be defended easily. Hanks and Sojda took on the task. They ascended to the roof of a house, and started looking south, as several planes dropped bombs nearby.

WHOOSH! An RPG streaked by them like a jet.

"Holy shit! Where did that come from?" Hanks asked Sojda.

The RPG landed about fifteen meters from 2nd Squad's Corporal Myirsky. Shrapnel hit the twenty-one-year-old corporal in the ankle, taking him out of the battle, while debris from the blast slightly wounded Gunny Hackett in the neck. No one could locate the muj who fired the rocket. Hanks and Sojda selected a house for the night, while Myirsky was medevaced to the battalion aid station. Out of its original strength of forty-five, 1st Platoon had already lost more than twenty-five men.

On November 12, 1st Platoon and the rest of Lima Company were pulled off the line and ordered to hold the area their battalion had seized over the past few days. Lima began to conduct "back clearing," military jargon for re-clearing the same neighborhoods they had cleared earlier. After studying the battle of Grozny (many of the Chechen fighters in Fallujah were probably veterans of Grozny), senior U.S. commanders realized they had to prevent re-infiltration of the ground recently seized.

The day was largely uneventful for 1st Platoon, but 2nd Platoon had one encounter with the enemy. A two-man sniper team engaged Staff Sergeant Van Daele and his squad of Marines as they swept through a cemetery filled with overturned graves and headstones. The muscular staff sergeant directed his Marines to outflank the snipers. The fight resembled a scene from a movie, as recorded in Van Daele's Bronze Star citation: "[Van Daele] courageously arose from his covered position, exposing himself to direct enemy fire, and, as rounds impacted around him, fired two shots directly into the head of one of the enemy insurgents, killing him instantly. As Van Daele continued his advance on the remaining insurgent, he threw a grenade into the enemy position, forcing the enemy to seek cover. This suppression enabled the flanking fire team to maneuver towards the enemy position, and engage the enemy, killing the remaining insurgent." Both "insurgents" were fair-complected foreign fighters wearing Vietnam-era "tiger striped" camouflage uniforms, a Chechen trademark. Intelligence later revealed that the Jolan and Queens districts were international terrorist bastions, dominated by al-Qaeda. Mujahideen in Fallujah hailed from eighteen different countries.

Shortly after Van Daele and his squad killed the sniper team, 1st Platoon was astonished to see several haggard, dust-covered men carrying a white flag, leading a procession of more than one hundred women, children, and older men. Several children were crying as they passed the Marines. "Sticking out like a sore thumb" were two twenty-something blond-haired men in Western clothes. They looked worn out, like they had just "run a marathon," recalls Conner. Hanks locked eyes with one of the men. "Where the fuck do you think you're going?" Hanks quickly handcuffed them with plastic zip cuffs he carried on his flak vest.

Sergeant Kyle, who had pulled embassy duty in Moscow, addressed the men in Russian. They concealed their faces by looking down at the ground, but their expressions revealed that they understood Russian.

"Chechens, intelligence warned us about them," said Kyle to Hanks. The Chechens were handed over to the HET team, and eventually taken back to the train station.

First Platoon selected a new shelter for the night, only to discover the house had been used as the company latrine the night before.

"Fuck no!"

Conner found an unsullied house for the men to sleep in. The squad moved into a bedroom lined with soccer posters, presumably belonging to an Iraqi boy, and collapsed. Everyone was sporting several days' stubble. Sojda and Hanks made a bed for Conner out of mats and grimy blankets. Exhausted, Conner pulled off his helmet and scrawled "LCPL LARSON" and "LCPL WOOD" on his digital helmet cover. The helmet cover was tattered by bullets and shrapnel.

"Hey, that's against regulations," Hanks smirked at Conner.

"If anyone bitches, I'll tell them to shove it up their ass," responded Conner as he turned over in his blanket.

The next day, November 12, turned out to be uneventful. Lima Company "back cleared" areas already swept by the battalion.

11

A Whiter Shade of Pale

This is another Hue City in the making.
—*Sergeant Major Carlton Kent*

A s FIRST PLATOON'S AMTRACKS CREPT DOWN A NARROW
stone road, Sommers, peering through his ACOG (telescopic
gunsight), saw something that didn't look right.

"Fucking stop! I think we have an IED."

Rosalez saw a battleship gray recoilless rifle aimed at the tracks.
The five-foot recoilless rifle was armed with an 80mm rocket that
could easily punch through an AAV's thin armor and cook everyone
inside. Black wires ran from the base of the weapon into a pockmarked house.

"Jordan, Suguitan, give me security."

Rosalez, a nimble Chicago native, climbed off the track,
inspected the rocket for booby traps, and snipped the wires leading
into the house.

Lance Corporal Jordan was white as a ghost. Nonchalantly,
Rosalez said, "Relax, devil, if it was going to go off it would have

detonated." Rosalez attached a one-pound block of TNT to the recoilless rifle, and demolished it.

"Good to go."

With the booby trap out of the way, the Marines dismounted from the tracks and pushed south along a sandy alley lined with half-destroyed houses, shops, and the occasional palm tree. On November 13, their fifth day in Fallujah, Lima Company's objective was to move south from Highway 10, or Phase Line Fran, to another road designated Phase Line Grace.

Conner took the point, with Hanks and Sojda following behind. As Conner moved down the alley, the men's heads swiveled back and forth 180 degrees, looking for the enemy and booby traps. Conner's eye locked onto a set of French wooden doors chained from the outside. Something wasn't right about the house. When Conner kicked the door, it didn't open, but the bottom half of the door split apart.

"There's someone in there," warned Sojda. "U.S. Marines, come out!" barked Conner.

"Gimmie a frag," said Conner. He turned around and found his head squarely in Sojda's chest. He didn't realize how close he was to the six-foot corporal, who readied a grenade as ordered.

Sojda decided to let the grenade "cook off" for two or three seconds so it wouldn't bounce back at them. He leaned his shoulder into the door. "One . . . two . . . Holy shit!" Horrified, Sojda looked down and realized the spoon on the grenade was cocked in the wrong direction and stuck on his right hand. He was a dead man if he did not act fast. With his free hand he wrestled the grenade out of his right hand and threw it into the room, where it exploded in midair.

The Marines heard screams. Sojda looked into the hole and saw a pair of feet running around. Conner began to fire his M16, and Sojda emptied an entire mag of hollow point rounds into the room. Hardin and Suguitan came up with an axe and beat the door down.

The grenade had kicked up a cloud of dust, so, for a few seconds, no one could see inside the tiny, four-by-four room. After the dust settled, Sojda found "a figure on the floor, its face is waxy from the hollow points, two grenades and an AK are laying next to it. From the eye to the forehead the skin was folded over and you could see the skull."

"That's a woman," said Corporal Adel "Abu" Abudayeh, a burly 2nd Squad fire team leader of Arab descent.

"No it ain't."

Abu removed the headdress covering the figure's head. The fighter was clearly a woman. He thought to himself, "What's next?" Nothing seemed sacred. If she had been an innocent civilian, she wouldn't have been armed to the teeth with grenades and an assault rifle. Moreover, she could have fled the city before the attack or surrendered earlier with the other civilians.

"Grandma Muj," someone else quipped.

The platoon broke through the chains on the back door, scaled a wall, and pushed forward. Third Squad took the right side of the street while the 2nd swept through houses on the left.

Led by Abudayeh, 2nd Squad entered a house not far from Grandma Muj. Abudayeh cleared a hallway, moved into the kitchen, and found a false wall. He pushed through it with his bare hands and saw a pristine Dragunov sniper rifle. Lying on the floor were a pair of Iraqi camouflage uniform trousers and a map. "It was the most beautiful rifle I'd ever seen, new in the case. As soon as I picked it up, the spoon for a grenade sprung."

Too late, he realized the rifle was connected to a wire.

"Shit!"

The rifle was attached to a hand grenade. *BOOM*. The entire kitchen was engulfed in flames, and its door banged shut from the blast as Abu ran through the doorway.

A second later, the door creaked open and Abudayeh staggered out of the room.

"Get out of the fuck out of the house!" he yelled. He limped toward the front door, and several Marines dragged him to safety. Lance Corporal Peterson recalled thinking, *"The cowards, using a booby trap. Why did he have to pick it up? He better not die. Just keep pushing."*

One of the men who rescued Abudayeh was Staff Sergeant Steven "Pyro" Bodek. It was the combat engineer's first day attached to 1st Platoon, but he had been in the battle from the beginning.

The day before, while attached to another 3/1 infantry unit, Bodek had witnessed firsthand the courage of a badly wounded Marine. Using an ACE (Armored Combat Earthmover) vehicle, which resembles a mini-tank with a dozer blade, the engineers were trying to collapse a building on a group of armed insurgents battling a squad of Marines. As the ACE's dozer blade cut into the building, the Marines took cover. However, when the building collapsed, part of it fell toward the Marines. Along with the jihadis, an American corporal was crushed. "The building broke in half and fell on top of him," recalled Bodek. Buried alive in the rubble, the corporal sustained massive injures: his pelvis, arm, ribs, and legs were broken.

Once the engineers uncovered the critically injured Marine, some of the first words out of his mouth were to Bodek:

"Staff Sergeant, I can't keep my promise."

"What is that?"

"I can't protect my Marines and get them home."

Bodek tearfully remembers the moment. "His body is totally mangled but he still had the guts to tell me that he couldn't keep his promise. I walked away and just bawled. I got down on my knees and just prayed to God."

When Abudayeh was wounded by the booby trap, Bodek stormed into the building. "Another lance corporal and I picked Abu up and ran outside with him. I yelled, 'Corpsman up!' And then we flipped him over. His back sappy plate was busted in four pieces." Abudayeh's head immediately started to swell from the concussion. The Marines quickly medevaced their injured comrade to safety.

Bodek yelled, "Gimme some grenades." Not knowing whether there were armed jihadis inside the building, he shouted, "You wanna throw grenades? *I'll* throw grenades."

"I took an entire ammo pack of grenades and started lobbing. They all went off. And I yelled to McFadden to bring up a Bangalore. When the "bang" went off there was a secondary explosion and the entire house went up, twisted in midair, and came back down."

With the loss of Abudayeh, 1st Platoon was running dangerously low on leaders. By this time the platoon had been reduced to two understrength squads. Undaunted, the Marines continued moving south. Nevertheless, it soon became clear there were too many houses and not enough Marines to clear them properly. According to Conner, "We had so many houses, we would first gain a foothold, get situational awareness, roll the next team past, and clear two structures at once. It wasn't the ideal way to do it, but we didn't have a choice." The men had to cut corners to get the job done.

Stokes recalls, "It was the worst day of the battle for me. After Abu got hit, it was just me, Kramer, Peterson, James, Barrickman, Huyett, and Sergeant Kyle and Lieutenant Sommers in 2nd Squad. That was it. There should have been fifteen-plus guys, plus support." Exasperated, Stokes turned to his squad leader. "I will do whatever you want me to do, Sergeant Kyle, but this is bullshit. We have no gun support, no security, no support team to clear these houses."

"It's just me, I'm the point man, and I'm going in first into every house. I'm not going to make it through this day."

Kyle was an effective leader who was respected by his men. He was a tough Marine, who led his squad the way Marine sergeants are trained: to coordinate the efforts of his men and direct their actions.

"I got your back. I will go in there with you," said Kyle.

"You got a kid, you're not coming in with me," replied Stokes.

"If you need support, I'll come," said Kyle.

Second Squad resumed houseclearing, but Stokes was on the verge of losing it. "Fuck this!" the private blurted. Then, suddenly, came deliverance.

"I was kicking down doors, and was really pissed, and then a miracle—two tanks assigned to one of the other companies rolled down the street. 'Thank you God, thank you God,' I prayed." Second Squad had several other kills. Butters had ripped a terrorist in half with his SAW at close range. He then emerged from the house with the terrorist's brains on his face and helmet, and quipped in his southern drawl, "I got me a hajji." Close combat in Fallujah was kill or be killed.

As the tanks rolled forward, several jihadis wearing Marine camouflage fatigues bounded across the street, running in a zigzag pattern to avoid fire.

"Hey, are those friendlies?" Several of the men looked through the ACOGs on their M16s.

"No they aren't."

"Shoot the motherfuckers."

Rosalez climbed up on the tank's turret and banged on the commander's hatch. Unfortunately, the Abrams field phone on the back of the tank, which allowed the infantry to talk directly with the tank commander without opening the hatch, was broken. The tanks were a temporary but welcome addition to the platoon's firepower. Usually, as Rosalez put it, "The SMAWs were our field-expedient tanks. The men had to improvise to survive."

At Rosalez's direction, the tanks blasted away at the muj fighters with their coaxial machine guns, while the Marines fired bursts from their M16s. One man dropped, and the others ran into a building. Tank rounds shredded the building, killing the jihadis. They were most likely Chechens, who were known for wearing Coalition uniforms, a clear violation of the rules of war.

Shortly after the tanks annihilated the camouflage-clad jihadis, a fighter popped out of a house, brandishing an AK, clenching his fist, and yelling in Arabic at Stokes.

"He had a detonator taped to his hand, so I double-tapped him in the face and he fell over," recalls the twenty-year-old private. The fighter was wearing a suicide vest and was prepared to martyr himself.

As 1st Platoon advanced down the rubble-strewn alley, they encountered a house with no windows, just a heavy metal door locked from the inside. Mark, an Iraqi interpreter who studied English at Baghdad University, urged the occupants to surrender. When they failed to reply, Bodek placed a block of TNT on the metal door. "Fire in the hole!" Seconds later the building was engulfed in a cloud of dust. The door was blown inward, flattening a jihadi like a pancake. After a few seconds came another tremendous blast. Huge secondary explosions sent debris flying for blocks. The house was likely an enormous booby trap that the muj planned to detonate after Marines had entered.

Throughout the afternoon, 1st Platoon was almost continually in contact with the enemy. Approaching yet another house, 2nd Squad relived the experience of the second day of battle.

"Mister, mister, come in." No doubt muj fighters were crouched on the other side of the closed door, machine guns trained on the doorway.

No one was taking chances. Stokes and the remnants of his squad waited as Mark tried to coax the jihadis to surrender. They ignored him, inviting an attack.

"I threw a grenade into the house and it landed on this guy's lap who was sitting on a couch. After the dust cleared we entered the house. The grenade blew him in half; his ass was sticking in the air," recalled Stokes.

Lieutenant Sommers strode into the room to inspect the damage. "What am I looking at?"

"His ass, sir," replied Stokes.

On the other side of the road, Hanks, Sojda, Conner, and Bryan ran into a house full of jihadis. Initially, the Marines gave them a chance to surrender.

"Americans—friends, come out," yelled Hanks.

"Americans—friends, come out."

"One guy came out. In the background, we heard loud whispering, and the sound of weapons locking and loading," recalls Sojda. "The one guy who was standing in front of us, maybe ten feet, we didn't want him to come in closer in case he had a bomb. The next guy who came out was armed and tried to fire at us. Conner yelled, 'Shoot!' The first guy dove back into the room for a weapon, so we killed both men."

"We didn't have the engineers, so blowing up the building wasn't an option. We pulled back from the road and two more guys came out with weapons in hand. Apparently they didn't see us. One was a kid, maybe fifteen or sixteen. He was carrying a weird Uzi or Tech-9, and we dropped both of them and moved on to the next house."

By midafternoon, sweat was dripping down everyone's faces; the stink of death permeated their nostrils. The platoon was nearly done for the day, fewer than one hundred meters from their objective—the next phase line. "For most of the morning, Bryan was acting different; he was a prankster, but he wasn't joking. It seemed like he knew he something was going to happen," recalled Sodja. Fighting exhaustion, 3rd Squad came to a house that appeared empty. They didn't know that a muj fighter had slipped in earlier.

Sojda recalls what happened next. "As we entered the house, Alavez and Lowe went upstairs with three or four CAP India Iraqis."

"Clear," yelled Alavez.

"Can I get a smoke from ya?" Sojda asked Bryan.

"Bryan reaches into his pocket to get a smoke, and hands it to me. As soon as I reach for the cigarette in his hand, I hear a twenty-round burst from an AK, full auto.

"The first couple of rounds miss Bryan. I saw them almost trace the outline of the doorframe, forming a rough square, I remember the tracers burning out the wall. I yelled, 'Oh fuck.' Just as I reached for Bryan's hand, I saw him spin around and hit the floor."

"Bryan, Bryan, are you okay?"

"He didn't answer, so I turkey-peeked around the corner and didn't see anyone. I popped around the corner again, and didn't see anyone, so I low-crawled out to him across the floor of the hallway. All of a sudden the guy popped up again, spraying his AK right at me. That's when my NVGs (night vision goggles) got shot off my web gear and shattered into ten pieces. The bullet was inside my deuce gear [web gear], on my left side, by my left kidney.

"'Holy fuck!'

"I could hear the AK rounds whizzing past me, snapping. I tried grabbing Bryan's foot as Marler, who was behind a wall, was sliding him into a room. I rolled out of the way of the incoming rounds. The guy was gone, we don't know where he went."

"Corpsman up!"

"Support up!"

"Where the fuck did he go?" yelled Sojda. Conner and Hanks and one of the platoon's two corpsmen, twenty-five-year-old Oliver "Doc" Escanilla, ran into the room. As they tended to Bryan, Alavez and Lowe searched the back yard and several houses on the block, but the elusive jihadi had disappeared. "A ghost," murmured Alavez. "He slipped in and out of here without a trace."

Bryan was hit in the soft side of his flak jacket, right in the seam between the front armor plate and the back armor plate. The bullet passed under his armpit, hit his heart and spine, and came out through his chest.

"I can't find a pulse!"

"Bryan's gone—he's gone!" stammered Doc Escanilla, tears welling up in his eyes.

"Fuck no, he's not gone."

"Run a pulse on him and get his ass stabilized," yelled Conner. A minute passed.

"I got a pulse, it's weak," responded Doc.

"We called for the ambulance to get him out of there. I tried to put a dressing on him. We put him in the track, and we moved as fast as we could back to the battalion aid station. I kept checking for his pulse. He died in my arms.

"I'm the corpsman, and I was there to save lives, but he died right in front of me." Escanilla's eyes teared up. "It's hard. They're not supposed to die when I have them."

"Their faces pop into my mind. At first you don't realize that they're dead. And then when you don't see them around, you realize that they're really dead."

Born in the Philippines, Oliver Escanilla, 1st Platoon's senior corpsman, was known for his bravery under fire. He was not alone. Medics and corpsmen were some of the bravest men in Fallujah. After the battle, nearly 150 corpsmen and medics, including Escanilla, were decorated for their valor. "The hardest thing for me to treat was Bryan because he had a sucking chest wound. I was wrapping special bandage and Ace wrap around him. I had to do this inside the tracks. The bullet went right along the edge of the sappy plate."

Sojda wiped his face and reflected on the moment. "I was just talking to him, asking him for a cigarette. I was holding his hand when he got shot. This is unreal, did that really happen? This isn't a game, this isn't anything to smile about, this is about life and death."

The men were worn out from another full day of combat. They went firm for the night in a large mosque, and the adrenaline began to drain away. Conner took a seat on a curb and was approached by Gunny Hackett. The two men did not speak on the gunnery sergeant to sergeant level; they spoke as two brothers, about the comrades they had lost to the city.

"Everywhere we go, we run into stuff," Conner said in a concerned voice. "Some of the other units are taking detainees, other platoons aren't running into shit. What are we doing wrong? We are doing what we are supposed to be doing, but we are just getting fucked."

Hackett saw Conner's morale needed to be built up. In his low, calming voice, Hackett responded, "We are not entering houses anymore without prepping with grenades or rockets, minimum a grenade."

"We are fucking Marines, this is what we do," said Conner.

For the next hour, all anyone talked about was Bryan. The little incidental things, his obsession with video games, and his ambition, when he left the Corps, to drive a beer truck. Bryan was "basic, he took one day at a time." He didn't let life become too complex. Most important, he was happy, something that most people only dream about achieving.

Everyone was disheveled and bearded, especially Conner, who was sporting his signature grunt look—with full beard, pant legs hanging outside of his boots, and obligatory dangling cigarette.

Even in combat, Marines are expected to look professional. Though the men were embroiled in one of the worst urban battles since World War II, one of the senior officers had ordered them to shave. Hanks smirked at the order, never missing a chance to take a jab at the chain of command: "Are we gonna die looking pretty?"

They somehow found a razor and cleaned up their faces. Conner shaved, but kept his trousers untucked; eternally a grunt's grunt, his heart remained defiant.

As the chatter of small arms fire and explosions echoed off the cavernous walls of the mosque, Hanks captured the moment on his video camera:

"Sojda, the last corporal in 1st Platoon. Wave, Sojda!" [Sojda waves and gets back to reading a letter from his wife.]

"That mail's not good enough for ya?" [Hanks laughs.]

"This is the old mosque we are in."

Conner walks by the camera with a cigarette dangling from his mouth. Hanks pans the camera over to Sommers.

"Lieutenant reading his porno—inside the mosque." [laughter]

Hanks's camera lingers on the growing pile of weapons left behind by 1st Platoon's wounded and fallen. Most of the weapons are "shredded" and pockmarked with shrapnel. "Day five of the old Falluj. Stack of weapons of the people we don't have anymore."

Gunny Hackett decided to inventory all the weapons and turn them in, rather than carry them around. Half the platoon was dead or wounded. Hackett and the others divided the bayonets, rifles, and NVGs into large piles.

"It was really hard," recalls Hackett. "I remember pulling out my roster to keep track, looking down at all the WIAs and KIAs. Oh my God. It hit me there. I got a job to do. I will mourn for these guys later. Right now, I have a job to do."

After the weapons were inventoried, what was left of 3rd Squad huddled around Hanks. Only Conner, Hanks, and Sojda, the best of friends, remained from the original group. Hanks pulled his worn CD out of his pack, and the haunting Vietnam classic, "A Whiter Shade of Pale" by Procol Harum, quietly played on the miniature speakers:

We skipped the light Fandango
Turned cartwheels 'cross the floor
I was feeling kinda seasick
But the crowd called out for more
The room was humming harder
As the ceiling flew away . . .

There was dead silence in the room. *This is what my dad went through as a Marine in Hue City. This is our generation,* thought Sojda.

"We all remembered those Vietnam clips of grunts staring off into space, looking at the floor, staring at their feet, tongues hanging out. That song was playing. We had not been together that long, yet we had come so far together and we got so tight with each other," recalled Conner.

12

"So Far Together"

Uncommon valor was a common virtue.
—Admiral Chester Nimitz

No one in the platoon knew it, but the Iraqi government declared Fallujah "secure" on November 13th. Like the great Pacific battles of Iwo Jima, Okinawa, and the Philippines sixty years earlier, politicians declared the battle won weeks before the fighting was actually over. The media echoed the Iraqi government's message. For the people on the ground actually doing the fighting, the reality was vastly different.

3/1's official chronology bluntly stated the real story on the 13th, the day Bryan died: "they continuously encountered pockets of determined resistance, eliminated only through violent close-quarters engagements with liberal use of supporting arms, to include armored bulldozers." Most of the assault force met the same determined resistance as it penetrated deeper into the city. Another week of hard fighting lay ahead.

The night of November 14th was white hot as the mujahideen advanced on Lima's go-firm base in the mosque. The sounds of battle were so intense that no one in the platoon could sleep. First Platoon, tasked with fire watch, or guarding the compound, was down to fewer than twenty Marines. However, the men had a powerful friend looking out for them: the AC-130U gunship nicknamed "Basher," the queen of the battlefield. Basher's mini-guns and cannon worked over the mosque's perimeter until dawn broke.

"That night was hellacious. Basher was almost firing inside our compound. I thought we were going to get overrun. It was up there for five hours lighting stuff up all around us. Nobody slept. There wasn't even a ten-second lull. I remember thinking, 'Holy shit, we are all going to die, this is Judgment Day,'" recalled Sojda.

That morning Conner broke out the Marine-issue face paint and applied a thick coat of black around his eyes, giving the impression he was wearing a mask. "The Ultimate Warrior," Conner joked. He looked less like the professional wrestler than the burglar from McDonalds. Hanks painted half his face white and applied black streaks like Mel Gibson in the movie *Braveheart*. Sojda put a black spot around his eye.

Painting their faces was their way of easing the tension of clearing houses. A touch of humor, and it looked tough. They felt bad to the bone.

"Hey, let me take a picture." Someone in the platoon took a snapshot of 3rd Squad made up for battle. Weariness from six days of fighting in the city was etched on their faces, as a large plume of smoke wafted out of Wade's nose. "Can you imagine the fear on a muj's face when he sees us?" someone said. It was their last picture together as a squad. Group pictures later became taboo because, according to Sojda, "Every time we took a picture, someone died."

After the photo, the men prepared for another day of clearing houses. Battalion HQ ordered Lima Company to push south into

"Queens," from Phase Line Grace, a road about a half-a-mile from Highway 10, to another road labeled Phase Line Heather. The entire area of Queens was a known terrorist stronghold. Al-Qaeda and its allies had kicked out the residents and set up shop in any house they wanted.

As 1st Platoon moved out from the mosque, they noticed the houses in Queens were bunched together, the roofs nearly touching one another. Sommers directed the platoon to clear from "roof to roof," sweeping from the top of the house to the street. Mixing up the platoon's clearing tactics helped keep the muj off balance.

Remarkably, the platoon's first contact was with civilians. A handful of people came out of a rubbled building and surrendered to the platoon. Sommers handed them over to 2nd Platoon, who had the duty of dealing with detainees. For a moment, the platoon felt like it was patrolling around the prison again.

As the detainees shuffled away, Garza noticed Baby, the youthful CAP India soldier, staring down the street like a zombie.

"Hey man!"

"Shit."

Crack! A round smashed into the street at the feet of Garza, Turpen, and Alavez. More rounds came whizzing from a house with a white flag draped from an upper story window. A black-clad muj came out of the house spraying bullets at Turpen, Baby, and Garza.

"He didn't make it across the street, I wasted him," remembered Turpen. Next, one of the terrorists did the unthinkable. "There was a guy with an AK trying to use a woman and a child as shields to cross the street." Once again, the terrorists had shrugged off the rules of war to gain an advantage over the Marines.

"That was the same MF that tried to kill me a second ago. Maybe it was the guy who killed Bryan. He's not going to get across the street," thought Turpen.

Once an enemy soldier uses a civilian as a human shield, the Marine rules of engagement (ROE) consider the civilian to be a combatant.

"Do I shoot, or not shoot?"

"I said, 'Fuck this,' and jumped into the middle of the street. 'Motherfuckers!'"

According to Alavez, "We had three guys from our squad killed. I remember the terp (interpreter) told us the women of Fallujah were evil. He took his finger and ran it across his neck like a knife, suggesting they'd kill you if you'd turn your back. We just had enough, plus once they used those people as shields they became combatants."

Turpen fired his SAW into the air. "I'm sure didn't I hit a damn thing." The group took cover in a building on the other side of the road. Clearing was hard enough; what with the Purple Hearts, the deaths of Larson, Wood, and Bryan, and now the enemy using civilians as shields, hatred burned brightly in the hearts of most of the men.

The platoon moved back onto the rooftops. The atmosphere in Fallujah was lethal, with random death always lurking nearby. "There wasn't a minute that passed day or night that there weren't rounds or explosions going off. On the roofs the shots were far away, you couldn't hear the shots, then WHOOSH, you'd just hear the rounds whiz by you," remembered Alavez. Most of the men ducked for cover as the rounds came in.

"What the fuck are you all doing? Fuck that." Conner stood up and pushed forward.

"Conner has balls," thought Alavez.

The squad followed the diminutive Irishman.

Most of the houses were empty, but not all. After the platoon cleared five or six houses, a hoarse voice croaked in broken English, "Marines, come down; I'm not armed, it is safe."

Over the radio, 1st Platoon had already heard that Marines from another company had fallen into a trap. Muj fighters lured the Marines into their building by offering to surrender, only to blow up the entire building and kill everyone inside.

Conner yelled back, "Drop your weapons and come out on the street!"

"Marines come down. It is safe."

In his southern drawl, Conner responded, "Whatta you talking about boys?"

Not fooled by the trap, Conner issued a decisive order.

"Frag out!"

With one fluid motion, the squad hurled grenades into the house. Next, "The engineers came up. They threw a satchel charge through a window and brought the whole house down," recalled Sommers.

After the dust settled, Sommers did a quick battle damage assessment and found three fully armed muj lying dead in the destroyed building. In the next block, the platoon encountered another fake surrender. Once again, the engineers blew the house, killing several terrorists.

By midafternoon, things seemed to wind down. Second Squad was leading the advance, with 3rd Squad in support on an adjacent street. Most of the houses were pockmarked but intact, with a few shredded palm trees adding a splash of green to the sandy-brown courtyard walls. Rubble littered the streets.

Lance Corporal Micah Huyett had point. As he crept forward, he put his fingers up to his mouth, shhh, and pointed his M16 at an open courtyard door. Then all hell broke loose.

"A barrage of bullets exploded from an open courtyard gate," Sommers recalled. A fusillade of enemy bullets sailed through the "fatal funnel" at Huyett. One round struck Huyett in the chest rig, hitting a magazine. Another muj bullet sheered off the tip of his left thumb and penetrated his thigh.

Instead of falling back, Huyett charged forward. "Die mother-fuckers!"

"Everyone seemed to freeze for a split second. Huyett got pissed off and unloaded an entire mag into the guys in the courtyard as he pushed through the left side of the door," recalled Slaughter. In near-perfect unison, the squad prepped grenades and threw them over the wall, incapacitating the muj.

"Fuck this, I'm going to get him!" yelled 1st Platoon's intrepid corpsman, Doc Tovar. "He did what we call the 'Medal of Honor Run,'" said Slaughter. "There were three insurgents in the courtyard, who shot Huyett in the leg. Doc ran across the opening, firing away with his 16, got to Huyett, and started bandaging him up."

"Hey, I'm going to put you in a fireman's carry," said Tovar.

"Fuck this, I can walk."

As Tovar pulled Huyett from the courtyard, Lance Corporal Peter Suguitan climbed up into an adjacent house overlooking the courtyard and expertly fired three DPs (dual purpose rockets, designed to take out bunkers and hard targets), finishing off any terrorists not killed by small arms fire.

As he limped away, down the alley toward the Humvee that would medevac him back to the battalion aid station, Huyett turned to Conner, who was providing security, and said, "Don't worry, I'll be back tomorrow."

Such scenes were repeated over and over in Fallujah. Men courageously risked death for one another. "The small heroics, it was daily. It became just like Admiral Nimitz said, 'Uncommon valor was a common virtue.' It was so common to hear or see a Marine praising another Marine for saving his life. It was, 'Oh yeah, good job. Keep going, we have another house to clear," recalled Gunny Hackett.

Huyett never returned to the battle. He was medevaced back to the United States along with the rest of Lima's seriously wounded, a quarter of the company.

As Huyett climbed into the Humvee, Stokes was on a knee, pulling security, covering the medevac. "All of a sudden, I see two hands and a rifle start shooting at a CAP India Iraqi in the street ahead of us. The fighter was firing like twenty yards ahead of me, shooting down the street. I took aim at him and missed him by an inch, hitting the cement right behind his head. Cement fragments and dust sprayed all over him. He turned around and shot at me, and I fell back behind a dirt mound. Then another guy with an RPK came out of a house closer to me. He puts the RPK on his hip and starts spraying, walking the rounds towards me. I was on the mound and my magazine goes dry. Right as my magazine goes dry and I'm changing it, the rounds are impacting closer and closer, and Corporal Yin shot him from behind me with a 40mm grenade launcher, vaporizing him into a cloud of blood and flesh."

On the other side of the block, Hanks spotted several muj fighters running into the remaining houses on the block. Conner quickly put the report on the radio. Everyone's head swiveled, looking for the enemy.

"We were getting reports over the radio of insurgents coming our way, when all of a sudden I see a guy in a black mask pointing his AK-47 right at me. That's when I put thirty rounds into the guy before he dropped. He fell down maybe twenty-five yards in front of me. After I pulled his mask off, his eyes were bloodshot and tan-colored and were real, real wide. He didn't look like a dead man," recalled Pyro.

In Fallujah, combat was up close and personal. The memory still haunts the tough Virginian. "It was the first guy I saw up close and I couldn't stop pulling the trigger. When I got home, I found out that no one understands, but the public needs to know what happened over there. These Marines fought, they gave everything they had. Eighteen- and nineteen-year-old kids not caring about dying. They didn't do it because they were ordered to do it; they were doing it for the guy standing next to you.

"At the time, I felt good about it. I was doing something to kill these bastards who are killing my buddies. But every night when you go home and lay down, you think about it. You see the guys' faces you shot."

About a dozen houses remained on each side of the block, twelve houses too many. The end of the day always seemed to be the most deadly time. Lima faced a highly motivated and disciplined enemy. "They knew what we were doing. It was always the last house on the last block when they would strike. They studied our tactics, sitting there, waiting to kill us before they died," said Sojda.

Gunfire erupted on the flank. Reports of 2nd Platoon, immediately adjacent to 1st Platoon, getting heavily engaged in a firefight, flooded the airwaves. Then Stokes engaged several muj. Those developments, combined with Hanks's report of seeing up to twelve armed muj fighters running into a courtyard in front of 1st Platoon, prompted Sommers to weigh his options. The platoon was down to only a handful of men. No civilians were spotted in the area. The muj may actually have outnumbered what was left of the platoon. The fighters owned this "hood," and maintained the element of surprise. The platoon was facing a hornets' nest.

"Volley fire with rockets. Level the block," Sommers barked to Slaughter, who was standing next to him. He issued a similar order over the radio to Pyro.

"I put about twenty-five rockets into the remaining houses on the block," said Slaughter, "while Staff Sergeant Bodek used about 200 pounds of explosives to eliminate the threat of the guys moving around.

"I made every Marine run to a different house with a security person and lay the charges down for a total of about twelve houses. Jack Rabbit was running around like a rabbit. All of the charges were attached to one firing device.

"*BOOM!* The entire block blew up in a massive explosion."

Miraculously, eight fighters emerged from the rubble, only to flee right into a tank attached to another Marine unit. The tank cut down three with its coaxial machine gun, while the rest escaped into the smoking ruins of Fallujah to fight another day.

13

Full Circle

Fallujah may not be hell, but it's in the same zip code.
—Unknown Marine

"WHY WOULD THEY PULL US OUT OF A WAR ZONE FOR ONE day of R&R?" mumbled Hanks. "Yeah, this has got to be fake, to lift our morale."

"Screw R&R, let's just do this and get it over with so we can have R&R for good," thought Sojda.

On the night of the 14th a rumor circulated that the platoon was about to be withdrawn from combat for a stint of R&R. The rumor turned out to be true; Lima would be pulled back to Fallujah's train station. The high number of casualties and the intense nature of the fighting persuaded the battalion CO to pull Lima off the line for a brief respite. Six days of intense combat had left every Marine exhausted. The men had deep five-o'clock shadows, eyes sunken into their faces, the thousand-yard stare.

After their tracks reached the train station on the morning of November 15th, the men slumped against the stark, concrete walls of the station's huge car barn. The men were proud, but worn out.

"The war movies never capture the pure exhaustion of battle. At the train station, we finally had time to think about happened over the past six days," recalled Conner.

It was at the train station that I first met the men of 1st Platoon. In their dirty, combat-worn camouflage fatigues, the Marines looked like combat veterans transported through time from the battle of Iwo Jima. After spending eight days with the intrepid warriors of 2nd Recon Battalion, who had conducted several dangerous and highly effective special operations raids in southern Queens, I felt even more honored to be joining the men who shattered the main line of resistance in the city. When I arrived in the station on the afternoon of the 15th, Lima's senior NCO, Gunnery Sergeant David Wilson, a former drill instructor, introduced me to the entire company. "This is Pat O'Donnell, he's our combat historian. He's here to tell your story." Even though they were completely exhausted, the men stood up and let out a massive "OORAH!" It was one of the proudest moments of my life.

I spoke first with Lieutenant Sommers, who introduced me in turn to Conner. At the time, the Leprechaun was listening to "bluegrass no one else wanted to hear." Conner told me some of his most vivid memories of the battle during his oral history interview, and later encouraged the grunts of 3rd and 2nd Squads to open up as well. Painfully the men revealed their impressions of the fighting. Most turned out to be eager to tell their story and honor the men who had fallen. They wanted America to know about the sacrifices they had made in Fallujah. One of the exceptions was Hanks, who simply said, "It's too soon." I knew that many WWII veterans still find it difficult to talk about their combat experiences, even after sixty years. I just nodded my head respectfully. Silently, I acknowledged that this Marine had seen a lot.

Later that day, the Marines were given an Iridium cell phone and allowed one five-minute call home. To gain the best reception, they stood on the top of one of Lima's Humvees. The officers led by example: officers and NCOs went last. The first man from 1st Platoon to use the phone was Private Stokes.

"Are you watching the news?" Stokes asked his parents.

"Yes, I see the Marines every day," responded his father.

"It's getting better, we are almost done. Today is my day off. I love you. Don't worry about me, worry about the guys we are up against," Stokes said with a straight face.

"Did you lose anyone?" asked Stokes's father.

"I have to go," Stokes responded, holding back tears.

Most of the platoon took their turns on the phone. Hanks told his girlfriend he loved her, and passed the phone to his best friend, Bill Sojda, who called his wife and parents. It was an emotional reunion.

"Good job over there."

"You're done now, right?"

"The news is saying the city is secure," said Sojda's mother.

"What? I don't think so, I don't know what the news is saying, but the city is not secure, that's not true," blurted the astonished corporal. Sodja told his family he loved them and passed the phone to the next Marine.

Many of the Marines were shocked when their families told them the press and Iraqi government had declared the city secure. The men were outraged at the reports, and some actually shook their fists, because they knew they would be going back into Fallujah the next day.

One of the last Marines to use the phone before the battery died was Staff Sergeant Bodek. "When I called my wife, she did not recognize my voice. She was crying after watching the news, which reported all the deaths. I said, 'Honey, don't worry about me. You know me, I'm hardheaded, I'll be home.' Next, I talked to my little girl, who was four years old at the time. She said, 'Daddy, when are you coming home?' 'Honey, I'll be home on your birthday, on April 1st.' 'Daddy, I love you; you do a good job and kill the bad guys.' My son, who was eight years old, told me that he got in trouble at school. He said he was standing in line at lunch and the principal told him to be quiet. He said, 'No, you be quiet, and if you pick on me, my daddy will come back from Iraq and hurt you.' I couldn't yell at him, but I just told him that you don't say that kind of stuff. I said goodbye to everyone and said, 'I love you very much; and no matter what, I will be coming home.'

"After handing the phone to the next Marine, I started thinking about all the Marines dying. It brought back all the memories of seeing Marines fall; it started to hit home. That night turned out to be the worst night of my life." Bodek began to choke up. "That was the first time I was scared that I may not come home."

Ironically, 1st Platoon was sharing a room in the car barn with many of the detainees whom the company had captured earlier in the battle. One of the Chechens started provoking Stokes. "He looked at me and wanted to kill me, so I went up to him and got in his face, talking shit in Arabic." A staff sergeant chased Stokes away from the detainee.

That evening, Captain Heatherman held a "lessons learned" meeting for the entire company. "This is your meeting, I hope to discuss what's working, and what's not," he said confidently. One of his first questions was, "How many of you are veterans of OIF I?" Over half the Marines in the crowd raised their hands.

"How does this compare to OIF I?" Heatherman asked.

"It doesn't, this is the shit," responded the tired Marines in unison.

Next, Conner discussed clearing tactics. Someone mentioned how rockets, Bangalores, and satchel charges had influenced the

Marines' tactics. "Do whatever it takes to get the job done," said Heatherman. "I don't want to lose anyone else." The meeting adjourned around 0700 and everyone turned in shortly afterward.

A rooster's crow, followed by a series of distant explosions, woke up most of the company on the morning of November 16th. After their first decent night's sleep in days, the Marines washed their faces, took a couple quick bites from care packages sent by a church back home, and ambled into their assigned tracks. The reduced 3rd Squad fit into a single track with plenty of room to spare.

"I'd like to roll with Conner," I asked Gunny Wilson. I'll never forget the stunned expression on his face. Wilson thought I was just collecting interviews at the train station. He was shocked that I was actually entering the city with the Marines. "The media always bugs out when the firing begins."

Wilson looked me straight in the eye and said, "Conner attracts the enemy." "I know," I responded, "but for the past month I've always gathered oral histories in the field and rolled with a rifle squad in combat." After shaking his hand, I climbed aboard Conner's track.

The high-pitched whine of the track's turbine engines tended to drown out conversation, so the men were quiet as the AAVs rumbled toward the city. Everyone seemed to go into a daze and retreat inside himself. The tracks were filled with cigarette smoke, and sunlight seeped in through open hatches. Some of the men were jittery and tried to mask their emotions by closing their eyes. The scene recalled troops in a Higgins boat making their way to the beach on D-Day, sixty years earlier.

The battalion's objective for the day was to "back clear" the same Queens neighborhood it had first cleared two days before, to root out any remaining pockets of resistance, destroy any remaining weapons caches, and make sure the muj had not reinfiltrated the area. The tracks chugged along down Fallujah's stricken streets, dodging piles of rubble. Most the buildings were destroyed or pock-marked with bullet and shell holes. First Platoon may have been returning to hell, but at least it was familiar ground.

Shortly after 1st Platoon dismounted from the tracks, a bedrag-gled man wearing a dirty white knee-length shirt came running up to Conner. Through an interpreter, the man claimed his son and another man were hiding in his house, but were afraid to surrender.

Conner suspected a trap, but decided to give the man the ben-efit of the doubt. The Marines pushed forward, following the man in the white shirt. Conner was behind him as they approached the gate of the house. The man called his "family" members to come out and surrender. They yelled back in Arabic that they were scared. Through an interpreter, Conner looked at the guy in the white shirt and bluntly stated, "Tell them to come out or I'll kill you. You have ten seconds."

The man called into the house and repeated Conner's demand. Seconds later, a teenage boy and another man filed out of the house with their hands up. Both men were escorted back toward the tracks. Through the terp, they explained that they were in Fallujah to visit relatives, and the guy in the white shirt was a dentist. Were they civilians, or mujahideen who had dropped their weapons? No one knew for sure, so they were sent back to the rear for further questioning by Marine Human Intelligence Exploitation Teams.

Combat on November 16th proved light for 1st Platoon. For the first time, a D9 armored bulldozer was attached to the platoon. The massive armored giant clanked forward, its huge polished steel blade and tracks smashing anything in its path.

Suguitan's two-man rocket team made its way to the roof of a three-story house and engaged a sniper. The remainder of the platoon was busy clearing houses, and, as they crossed the street, an RPK opened up. One of the platoon's machine gunners, Lance Corporal Baker, scrambled forward to lay down suppressive fire. Suguitan quickly silenced the RPK with a rocket.

A few hundred meters farther south, the men began to take fire from a sniper in the minaret of a mosque. Staff Sergeant Bodek's combat engineers leveled the minaret. Post-battle analysis would reveal that over half of Fallujah's ninety-nine mosques had been used as fighting positions and arsenals.

That afternoon, Lieutenant Zach Iscol's Combined Action Platoon (CAP) India, rather than Conner's 3rd Squad, seemed to be attracting the enemy. From the moment they captured the train station on the night the battle began, CAP India had performed brilliantly, becoming one of Iraq's most successful post-Saddam units and a model for the Iraq National Guard.

CAP India was created in 2003 by the 82nd Airborne Division's 505th Parachute Infantry Regiment, the unit occupying Fallujah before the Marines. When the unit was transferred to the Marines, it consisted of approximately 280 Iraqis and 27 Marine instructors fighting alongside them. Most of the men were from a single Fallujah suburb, Nasser Wa Salaam, a Shiite island in Sunni-dominated Anbar Province. Years before the war, Saddam's government had transported the Shiite families from the south to work in Fallujah's industrial sector.

Iscol's Marines worked with the Iraqi volunteers for five months, molding them into a cohesive fighting unit. Several weeks before the battle, Iscol and the Iraqi major in charge of the unit literally drew a line in the sand and asked who wanted to fight with the Marines in Fallujah. "Most of the company volunteered," recalls Iscol. The Marine instructors handpicked forty of the Iraqis. "Our focus became preparing these forty soldiers. After five months of working with these guys, you see who doesn't complain, who wants to be with us. In the end, it was about personal relationships." The initial group of forty was eventually whittled down to about thirty men, who went through intensive physical training and live fire exercises in preparation for the battle.

Joining CAP India was an act of pure courage. Nearly every single man in the unit, and their families as well, received death threats. The mujahideen run a very effective intimidation campaign, which remains one of their most effective weapons in oppressing the Iraqi people. In many ways, the Sunni insurgents and foreign terrorists have stepped into the shoes of Saddam's secret police, who had terrorized Iraqis for decades. Of course, many of the insurgents are former members of Saddam's secret police. The mujahedeen even managed to penetrate CAP India and kill several of its soldiers. Despite the risk, CAP India soldiers courageously continued to volunteer and train with the Marines.

That afternoon, CAP India's truck section, the men who transport the unit into battle, came under fire while traveling into Queens on a resupply mission. The Marine truck drivers dismounted and threw several grenades into the building the shots came from. The grenades did not find their mark. The sniper popped up, sprayed the Marines with bursts from his AK, then picked up an RPG and prepared to fire at a Humvee. "Twenty-year-old Lance Corporal Louis Wayne Qualls bravely ran around the far side of the building to attack the jihadi. Qualls flushed him out, preventing him from firing at the Humvee, but as he was fleeing from the building he shot wildly and hit Qualls in the face," recalled Iscol.

Like Hanks, Qualls did not have to be in Iraq. He had recently started college but dropped out to protect his friends who joined the Corps. Qualls volunteered four times before he was finally accepted into the service. Before he left for Iraq, he told his father, "I couldn't go to Iraq without watching their backs."

Shortly after Qualls fell, CAP India Marines stacked outside of a house near 1st Platoon. "Frag out!" The grunts hurled several grenades through an open window. Before the grenades detonated, a bearded terrorist inside the house attempted to blow up himself—and the Marines—with an improvised explosive device (IED) hidden in a refrigerator. Fortunately, the bomb failed to detonate, and the grenades killed the terrorist. Bodek's engineers blew the IED in place.

Just before sunset, 1st Platoon went firm for the night in a walled stone house. As the men scrounged around for blankets and mats, CAP India joined the platoon in their makeshift camp, and some of the Marines finally had a chance to talk with the Iraqis they had been fighting with.

One of the first people they spoke with, through Mark, CAP India's "terp," was Baby, the youngest Iraqi soldier in the unit. "How old are you?" "I'm eighteen. Nineteen."

Baby looked like he was barely out of puberty. Everyone doubted he was even seventeen. But Baby was a good soldier who followed orders, so the Marines liked having him around. "I got my courage here. The Marines have trained me well. Before I joined the Marines, I was afraid of the war. I have the courage now."

"Why are you fighting?"

"I'm fighting for my country," Baby responded with firmness and sincerity.

Reluctantly, one of Baby's Iraqi NCOs joined the conversation. "We are finally free from the tyrant Saddam, now we are fighting against terrorism. The terrorism is all over the world. My family and I been threatened by the terrorists; they delivered pieces of paper to my house telling us they'd execute us. Our aim is peace in Iraq."

Major Aouda, CAP India's ranking Iraqi officer, was a veteran of the Iran-Iraq War and the first Gulf War. Aouda deserted from Saddam's army during OIF I and joined CAP India when the unit was formed. "His picture and his name have been called from all the mosques. He's been shot at. His family has been shot at. They've kidnapped his son a number of times, forcing the family to move. He's one of those Iraqis who is making enormous sacrifices, he's a great man," said Iscol proudly.

"I didn't agree with [the Iran-Iraq War]," said Aouda. "I saw the mass executions, the killings. Everybody that lived through that war has a hard time accepting the events that took place. It's my good luck that I'm alive today.

"I'm proud of these men and their courage. I've never seen anything like it. This is a battle of the streets and far more difficult than the front lines of the other wars I've been in. I wish to end my service with these guys.

"I'm a man of peace. I'm looking for peace. I hope that those trying to stop the elections and democracy here fail."

That night everybody slept in his armor. Numerous RPGs, mortars, and small arms rounds were slamming into the walls and sides of the building as the mujahideen attempted to overrun the house. Basher was lighting up the area all night. The battalion air officer orchestrated attacks on twenty-four targets. Between the Marine jets and the AC-130U, twenty of the targets were destroyed. After surviving the night's maelstrom, 1st Platoon awoke to what would be their worst day in the city.

14

The Wolves of Islam

*If the wolf loses the struggle, he dies silently, without expression
of fear or pain. And he dies proudly facing the enemy.*

—*Chechen myth*

A S THE MEN AWOKE ON NOVEMBER 17, things were surprisingly quiet. Lima Company's objective was to push farther
south into Queens, from Phase Line Heather to Phase Line Isabel,
clearing more city blocks of mujahideen. Only nineteen of 1st Platoon's original forty-five Marines remained standing.

CAP India's Iraqis were resting near the platoon. As the
Marines munched MREs, three CAP India Iraqis, clad in the old-
style U.S. fatigues from the Gulf War, passed by, pushing a large tire
from a tractor trailer truck. Nobody knew where they were taking
the tire, or why, and they were unable to explain it to the Americans.
Their English vocabulary was limited to words of the four-letter
variety.

"Fuck you," said one of the Iraqis, smiling.

"Fuck you too."

Before 1st Platoon pushed off, the only person talking was
Lance Corporal Michael Hanks. The rest of the men were huddled

on the stone steps leading to the alley in front of the go firm house. Rap music played softly in the background.

That day, perhaps more than any other, the natural storyteller in Hanks rose to the surface. Everyone was exhausted, but he was funny and interesting. As he regaled the platoon with one of his off-base exploits, he repeated the famous Matthew McConaughey line from the movie *Dazed and Confused*: "I get older, but the girls stay the same age."

Eventually, the monologue took a serious turn. Hanks said, "I consider these people spies, they wear civilian clothing, exploit our ROE by dropping their weapons and running to another weapons cache. The rules to fight this war need to change."

Because of political pressure in the aftermath of the Abu Ghraib Prison scandal, many of the muj captured in Fallujah were eventually released, and given the opportunity to kill again. Perhaps the most infamous released detainee was Safaa Mohammed Ali. Captured by U.S. forces during the battle of Fallujah, Ali was released two weeks later because his captors failed to identify him correctly as a combatant. Nearly a year, later he would detonate a suicide vest and murder fifty-seven people attending a wedding party in Amman, Jordan.

Hanks never talked about his exploits on the battlefield, like the time when he rescued an Iraqi girl from a burning building during Operation Iraqi Freedom I, or when he carried Sergeant Alvarado out of a firefight a few days earlier. He had avoided so many close brushes with death that many of the men privately thought he was "bulletproof." The men in the platoon considered Hanks a hero.

Hanks's most impressive quality was his sense of duty. Most of the Marines in 3rd Squad had made it this far thanks to Hanks and Sojda, who had extended their terms in the Marine Corps so they could continue to protect the younger, less-experienced men in their squad. The younger Marines, eighteen and nineteen years old, had been taken under the experienced wings of twenty-two-year-old Hanks, twenty-two-year-old Sojda, and the old man, twenty-eight-year-old Sergeant Conner.

Garza remembered Hanks putting his hand on his shoulder shortly after Larson was ambushed on November 9, and saying, "I'm not going to let anything happen to you. I'm going to get you home alive."

Before the platoon pushed south, Sergeant Conner stood silently, head down, in a reflective trance that lasted five minutes. Conner was thinking about the three Marines in the squad who had already fallen—Nathan Wood, Nick Larson, and Benjamin Bryan. A sense of foreboding was gnawing at his belly; he sensed something big was about to happen.

Meanwhile, Hanks was joking with Sojda. "They still haven't gotten my tooth." Smiling, he pointed to the false tooth replacing the one he lost in a street fight.

Around 10:00 a.m., the platoon started driving toward Phase Line Isabel, clearing houses of jihadis.

Soon, Kramer's 203 coughed, and his grenade blew the gate off a walled courtyard in front of the platoon. The clearing continued, with the staccato crackle of small-arms fire in the distance. All of sudden, everyone's eyes and nose started watering. "It's CS riot gas." Bodek quickly confirmed that the insurgents had uncorked the odorless gas. Both squads pulled back a bit and waited for the gas to drift by.

The platoon passed by the "house of the dead," where three muj had made a last stand. The bodies of the fallen men lay next to the house, their faces twisted into grotesque grimaces. One fighter was wearing a modern chest rig, and several of the rig's magazine pockets had taken direct hits, causing the bullets to explode in the harness. Half his face had been removed by a large caliber projectile. His hands were stretched in the air like he was reaching for something. His lips were gone, eaten by the dogs. Next to him, another jihadi wearing a blue-gray *dishdasha,* the Arab men's shirt that hangs past the knees, lay in a pool of his own dried blood. His body was sprawled in the threshold of the doorway to a courtyard. Ironically, an olive branch was lying across his chest.

"The doorway to death," someone murmured.

The third man's body rested near the street beside a stone wall, a ball-shaped British Mills grenade lying next to his outstretched hand. Apparently he was attempting to hurl it when he was cut down. Flies swarmed over the bodies. The stench of death permeated the air.

Moving south, the platoon passed several walls bearing stick figures drawn by children. Several men flashed back to their childhoods.

Just like playing guns.

Surprisingly, the funniest man in the platoon had gone silent. Hanks wasn't cracking jokes or even smiling as the squad cleared buildings. "Mike wasn't himself, I think he knew something was going to happen," recalls Sojda. Hanks's presentiment was right. The platoon was about to get into its worst fight of the entire battle, a sophisticated ambush prepared by highly trained Chechen soldiers.

The Chechens in Fallujah were ruthless Islamic jihadists, the self-proclaimed "Allah's warriors" whose openly stated objective is to create a radical Islamic state in southern Russia. Their national symbol is the wolf. Their pack leader was Shamil Basayev, a "Che Guevara-like" one-legged terrorist who lives in Chechnya's caves and forests.

Before he was killed by a Russian Special Forces Unit in 2006, Basayev was a living legend, and an infamous cold-blooded killer.

He was aligned with al-Qaeda and supported financially by Osama bin Laden. Basayev has hijacked airliners, deployed "black widow" female suicide bombers, orchestrated the infamous slaughter of school children and noncombatants at Beslan, and carried out the first-ever act of nuclear terrorism. In 1996, Basayev smuggled a dirty bomb made of Cesium 137, a highly radioactive isotope, into a busy Moscow park, and threatened to turn the city into a "radioactive desert." He didn't detonate the bomb, but the threat forced the Russians into peace talks.

As 1st Platoon had already confirmed from bitter experience, intelligence reports warned that the Wolves were wearing "tiger stripe" camouflage fatigues used by American Special Forces in Vietnam. Kilo Company's CO, formerly a military observer in Chechnya, even reported overhearing jihadis speaking Russian. Postbattle intelligence revealed that the Chechens typically operated in small teams, leading the Marines to surmise that they were teaching their tactics to muj units fighting throughout the city.

After moving past a lengthy series of empty buildings, 1st Platoon came to a house resembling a dog kennel, with broken cages strewn all over, and passed through to an open area. Complacency was beginning to set in when the eerie silence was broken by Second Lieutenant Jeffrey Sommers's commanding voice. "There's a motherfucker running around!"

Sommers saw a man jumping over a courtyard wall near a red gate, and pumped several rounds into him. "I'm either a terrible shot or he was high on adrenaline, since he kept moving through the courtyard."

Sergeant Conner dashed toward Sommers and shouted, "Let's get that bitch!" The rest of the squad started throwing grenades into the courtyard, which led to a pair of connected buildings.

"Is anyone going to check if the motherfucker is dead?" Conner wondered. He kicked open the gate and crept carefully into the empty courtyard, with Hanks following. "I guess the guy avoided the grenades and jumped the wall." Conner and Hanks pushed farther into the courtyard, "snooping and pooping like our lives depended on it."

Hanks looked at Conner and said, "Fuck this, dude, I'm tired of seeing our guys getting killed." According to Conner, "Hanks and I made an agreement: if anyone else gets hit in the squad, it's going to be one of us. I wanted it to be me rather than him, and I think he was thinking the same thing."

The platoon was deployed in an L-shape. Second Squad was on the western side of a group of buildings, and 3rd Squad was in an alley facing the buildings from the south.

Sergeant Kyle ordered Heath Kramer to take his fire team and clear one of the houses.

"Peterson, Stokes, and Damico—let's go."

"Good to go," the Marines responded.

"We walked toward the first door of the house," recalled Peterson. "We got in the foyer. Stokes and I were the first ones in the house. Stokes was on point in the first room that we cleared. There were four open doors, a stairwell, and one closed door. It was a black door on a black wall. It was the creepiest looking thing I've ever seen. Stokes and I looked at this door, and we both said, 'We'll save that one for last.' Stokes gets ready to charge into the room with the black door and I'm right behind him—just like always."

Then the black door began to open.

"What the—!"

"Stokes, get the fuck back!" yelled Peterson.

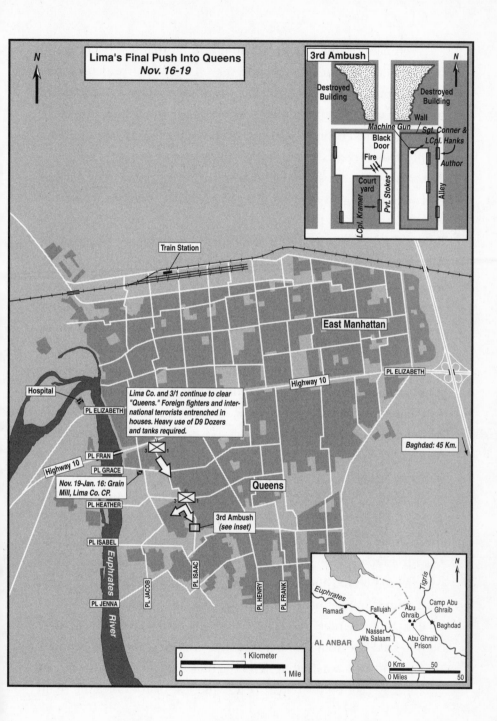

Lima's Final Push Into Queens
Nov. 16-19

3rd Ambush

Destroyed Building

Destroyed Building

Wall

Machine Gun

Sgt. Conner & LCpl. Hanks

Black Door

Fire

Author

Court yard

Pvt. Stokes

LCpl. Kramer

Alley

Train Station

East Manhattan

PL ELIZABETH

Hospital

PL ELIZABETH

Highway 10

Lima Co. and 3/1 continue to clear "Queens." Foreign fighters and international terrorists entrenched in houses. Heavy use of D9 Dozers and tanks required.

Baghdad: 45 Km.

PL FRAN

PL GRACE

Highway 10

Nov. 19-Jan. 16: Grain Mill, Lima Co. CP.

PL HEATHER

Queens

3rd Ambush *(see inset)*

PL ISABEL

PL ISAAC

Euphrates River

PL JACOB

PL HENRY

PL FRANK

PL JENNA

0   1 Kilometer

0   1 Mile

Euphrates

Tigris

Ramadi

Fallujah

Abu Ghraib

Camp Abu Ghraib

Baghdad

Nasser Wa Salaam

Abu Ghraib Prison

AL ANBAR

0 Kms   50

0 Miles   50

Peterson recalled, "You talk about things that will haunt you. I will remember that door for the rest of my life. I remember the adrenaline rush and the fear that hit me all at once. When I heard the door creak open and saw the AK creep out, that is one thing that I will never forget. I start shooting and the AK opens up on both of us. Tracers barely miss us, no more than five feet away. Tracers go past us: *swish, swish, swish!* They are going right between our legs. I kept shooting at the muzzle, and saw a mist of blood, I think I got the guy's hand. The AK jerks back into the door and a grenade rolls out. At that moment, we didn't see the grenade because it was too dark. The next thing I know, the grenade explodes no more than five feet in front of both of us. Don't ask me how or why, but it must have been divine intervention that we weren't blown up. I got about five or six pieces of shrapnel. If you've ever been popped with a rubber band really close—that's what it felt like. Like somebody took five rubber bands and popped me right in my face. The blast was hot, the metal was hot. Kramer saw what happened, later he said that the blast went right through me. I took the brunt of the explosion; I kept popping rounds into the room."

The blast blew Stokes, who was standing near Peterson, into the kitchen. "The grenade blew up within five feet of me. It was like being hit with a bowling ball. I took four to five pieces of frag from it. As I tried to stand up, I felt totally helpless and claustrophobic. As I tried to run one way, my head was going the other way. I could not hear anything and I just looked up at the wall, and saw tracers and rounds impact near me. I thought I was going to die."

In Stokes's opinion, "The Chechens were well trained; they suppressed the room and tossed the grenades out in a textbook manner. Kramer was yelling, 'Get the fuck out!' If we had stayed, we would have gotten torn apart. I was the last man exiting the room

172

when a second grenade rolled past me and blew up." The concussion knocked Stokes down again. "Everything happened so fast; as I was getting to my feet, I was woozy; my equilibrium was messed up pretty bad. I remember trying to run down the hallway. The door out of the house was locked. I remember kicking the door, but I fell down because I was all woozy. As I got up, rounds started impacting near me down the hall. They kept coming closer, closer."

The team ran out of the house, thinking Stokes was right behind them. Kramer started looking around. "Where the hell is Stokes?" asked Kramer.

"He is right here," responded Peterson.

"Oh shit!"

In fact, Stokes had stumbled into another room, and was engaging the Chechens by himself. "I was firing at the Chechens who were getting closer, when my magazine went dry! Everything I did was by instinct, so I pulled out a grenade to frag the Chechens. I thought I was going to die; I was out of mags and they were just about to peek around the corner."

The fire team heard the gunfire inside the house, and then heard Stokes scream "No!"

"Stokes is over there," Peterson yelled.

Damico started to lay down suppressive fire on the house with his SAW (squad automatic weapon), and Kramer prepared to go back in, yelling, "Stokes! Stokes! Stokes!"

The Chechens came out from behind the door, threw another grenade, and started shooting at Stokes.

"I didn't see him and he didn't come toward me," recalls Kramer. "I just stuck my muzzle around the corner where the Chechens were and I started shooting blindly. I got ten or fifteen rounds off. Damico and Peterson ran back inside the house. Damico was spraying his SAW.

"Stokes was located in a room behind a large, rough-looking door. The adrenaline was pumping, I took a running start and bull-rushed it. Thankfully, it opened up."

"Let's get the fuck out of here!" blurted Kramer as he picked up the stunned Marine and helped get him moving. Stokes recalled, "If you remember the movie, *Saving Private Ryan*, there's that scene where he is lying on the beach and he doesn't hear anything. That's how I felt when Kramer and I were getting out of the building. As I was walking, I realized I was dripping blood with a piece of frag in my leg. Doc patched up my hand and they sent me to the Humvee."

Once 2nd Squad was clear of the house, the combat engineers accompanying 1st Platoon got into the fray. According to Bodek, "There were large amounts of fire, as grenades were thrown at us. We all fired into the house, suppressing the enemy. Then Jack Rabbit and I moved closer to try to get a better shot at the enemy through a window. Shots came at us through the window and Roberts came running out the back of the house, being chased by the rounds."

Tanks arrived on the scene, but Bodek was having none of it. "I said, 'Tanks, hell no. Now you've fucked with the wrong engineers!' Bodek and Jack Rabbit crawled up to the wall, primed a Bangalore, crawled back to the street, and ran for cover. "No sooner had we turned the corner when the house blew sky high, only one tiny portion remained standing. The grunts were cheering us."

At the same time 2nd Squad was being ambushed, Sergeant Bennie Conner's 3rd Squad was drawn into an ambush on the opposite side of the buildings. I was accompanying 3rd Squad.

Conner recalled how it happened: "I went walking up to this southern wall of the house. There were a couple bricks missing that I could get through, so I pushed the wall in and Hanks follows me.

At this point, I'm not sure where the rest of the squad was at. The next thing I came up to was a window, and I came face-to-face with a fighter. This son of a bitch looks like Yasser Arafat in his younger days. He had a red towel on his head. He had a dirty, dark-green coat on. I raised my weapon to shoot him through the window, but the ground was at a slope and you know I'm only 5'3". I didn't have a good shot. If I pulled the trigger, I would have shot the ceiling. I was going around to the door to get a better shot. I guess this guy heard me. He just spun around and pulled the trigger on his RPK. I thought to myself, '*Shit!*' I dropped to the ground. It felt like someone socked me in the arm, and I spun around. I remember talking to myself and wondering if I was dead. I backed up and looked down at my arm and saw some red—I didn't realize how bad it was until later." Conner had at least one bullet in his upper arm and a fragment in his forearm.

"Hanks, watch out! I'm hit, I'm hit!"

Hanks yelled back, "Conner's hit!"

"The whole time, he is watching my back, so I come around the door and there is nobody in there," recalled Conner. "I'm so pissed off, I empty a magazine in the room. As I was doing this, I noticed the guy I was fighting had a weapons cache. He had two RPGs, an SKS, and a couple of AKs. It wasn't enough for an army, but it was enough for one or two men to wreak some havoc."

Conner called out to Hanks, "I'm hit, dude, I got to come by this window, so cover me."

Hanks yelled back, "Okay, dude."

"I rolled under the window. Hanks, he had good cover; he was behind a wall. He was looking over the wall towards me."

"Come on, dude, get the fuck out of there," shouted Hanks.

The next moment replays endlessly in my mind's eye. I was crouching behind the wall next to Hanks. A presence I can't explain told me, "Don't go any farther, you aren't trained to clear a house." I hesitated for a second, but Hanks didn't.

Suddenly a massive volume of RPK fire came out of the building. Then I heard someone yell, "He's gone! Corpsman!"

"Hanks is fucking gone!"

Michael Hanks's bloody head was lying next to my boot.

There were still a lot of bullets flying, but for a second everyone stopped. The moment seemed to last for an eternity. Then everyone was snapped back into action by the Platoon Commander's orders. Sommers decided to avoid any further casualties by bringing in tank support. He barked, "Get Hanks, get him outside. A tank will fucking level this."

Gunny Hackett grabbed the platoon radio. "I have a priority medevac. Break. I'm at grid 8643 8929."

They started pulling back, firing and throwing grenades at the house. Since I thought there was a tiny chance Hanks was still alive, I grabbed the back of his flak jacket and started dragging him to the rear. A Marine came to help me.

As the squad was moving back, Conner escaped the courtyard through another gate in the wall and caught up with them. Unaware that Hanks had been hit, he said to the entire squad, "There was a hardcore muj in there. He had the fucking headband and everything and was positioned behind a large weapons cache with an RPK." Conner's arm was soaked in blood. I remember him ripping off his uniform's sleeve, still firing his M16 and directing the squad.

A tank arrived to provide fire support. Despite the blood spurting out of his arm, Conner told the tankers where to fire. "That house right there needs to go away!"

As the tank shredded the building, Sergeant Conner and the remaining members of 3rd Squad pulled back about one hundred meters, crossed a road, and made their way to a walled compound where the wounded were being treated. Conner, Lieutenant Sommers, Corporal Hardin, and Garza had all been hit. I was dragging Hanks with my right arm. Hanks's lifeless body weighed a ton.

"The next thing I know," Conner recalls, "they are trying to get me situated, and that's when you brought Hanks's body back, and he didn't have a face. I remember saying, 'Who the fuck is that?' and I knew who it was. I just didn't want to admit it."

Conner poked at Sojda and said, "Bill, talk to me, dude."

"Is that fuckin' Mike?"

"Is that fuckin' Mike?"

Sojda's eyes were as big as saucers as he nodded up and down. Conner beat his hands on the dirt courtyard and said, "No, motherfuckers!" A tearful Sojda picked up his best friend's bloody helmet and weapon.

Stokes was also on his way to the compound to be medevaced. "I remember walking down the street and seeing you dragging somebody down the street. I said to myself, *'Who the fuck got hit?'* The second before, I was just so happy to be alive. I remember telling Kramer, 'You saved my life, I'm so happy to be alive right now. I'm so happy to see you.' How I only took five pieces of frags with that grenade blowing up with nothing in between me and the grenade. I could have kicked the grenade, that's how close it was. I still couldn't believe I was alive. Then when I saw Hanks's body, I was like, *'What the fuck?!'* I thought Hanks was bulletproof, like he could never be killed. Then, when I saw him, it was a really weird mix of emotions."

Gunnery Sergeant Wilson, Lima Company's top Staff NCO during the battle, arrived at the compound to check on the men. "I walked up to 1st Platoon. Sojda has Hanks's helmet in his hands. He's got this look on his face that I had not seen on anyone's face, yet. We had dealt with death already, but here you're talking about a guy's best friend, and Sojda was carrying his best friend's helmet. You couldn't read the name on the back of the helmet because there was so much blood. Sojda was just wandering. I let him keep walking, but I felt compelled to take the helmet out of his hands. I went up to him and gently said, 'Let me just take that.' I couldn't imagine losing my best friend, being in that situation, so I took the helmet and for whatever reason—I felt compelled—I needed to clean it. So, I got a bunch of water bottles and I cleaned it off. The next time he went for the helmet, I didn't want it to be covered in blood. It was full of blood—it was a bucket of blood. I cleaned it out as best as I could—cut off the liner, took off the helmet cover and got rid of all that stuff. Then I put it on the truck. Sojda handled the experience incredibly well. Sojda stayed dignified and he pushed forward. That's a warrior."

Someone said Conner needed medical attention for his arm. Despite his serious wounds, Conner still had plenty of fight left in him.

"I'm not leaving my fucking Marines!" he shouted. "They oughta just napalm this fuckin' place!"

"Right now, I know how you feel, but we got to get you back to the aid station," replied Gunny Hackett.

According to Conner, "Doc Escanilla was trying to bandage me up and put me in an ambulance. Once I made sure everybody was holding security, and everything was settled down, I said, 'Hey, can I get a fuckin' pressure bandage?' It's kind of funny, because Doc E was trying to help me the whole time. Doc bandaged me and they loaded me into the ambulance. They also placed Hanks in there and I didn't want to even look at him. I had already seen what he looked like, and I tried to forget about it really quick."

Stokes also resisted evacuation. He told Sergeant Kyle, "I don't want to go back, I'm fine, I'm fine. I don't want to leave." The corpsman decreed that he had to go, because he was so badly concussed that he couldn't remember his Social Security number. "Wounded, almost dying from a grenade, and seeing his buddy get killed by the Chechens in the house, and Stokes still wanted to stay in the battle," recalls Kyle. "It says a lot about him as a Marine."

Sergeant Daniel Tremore from 3rd Platoon tried to spare Hanks's friends from having to handle the fallen Marine's gear. "I was going through [3rd Squad's equipment] with Sergeant Kyle to make sure they had all their stuff and then they pulled Hanks's weapon out. You can't have somebody in their platoon clean it, it's just bad. It's very bad for morale to have them clean it up and see what happened. I ended up taking Michael Hanks's weapon and cleaning it. For me, that was the worst moment of the entire battle. Everything went numb for a minute. You don't hear any of the sounds of battle, you don't see anything, everything becomes slow motion. The blood was running off and I was scrubbing parts of him off his weapon. It took probably four or five bottles of water and I'm scrubbing with a brush, pieces of him and his blood, and it's running onto me, running on the ground. The worst thing was having to rescrub it over and over again.

"It's pretty unbelievable. You hear what it's like to see a friend killed, but until it actually happens, it doesn't really dawn on you. At that point in time, it becomes real, since you're actually dealing with it face-to-face. You can't ignore it; it sticks in your head and makes everything pause."

As the Humvee carrying Sergeant Conner and Mike Hanks's body pulled away, a remarkably composed Corporal Bill Sojda assumed command of what was left of 3rd Squad. The men's faces were ashen, their eyes filled with tears. Lance Corporal Jacob de la Garza, the last surviving member of Hanks's fire team, covered his head with a brown scarf. Garza was spent. His face looked like he had aged ten years, and he said nothing to his buddies. Lance Corporal Steven Wade grabbed his hand and said, "Garza, we'll get you home."

The remaining men in the squad held hands. According to Derick Lowe, "It was our way of silently saying, *We came through this, we are going to make it out of here together, no matter what happens.'* We were all dropped into 3/1 together around the same time, and for most of us the squad was the brothers we never had. When one hurts, you all felt it."

As the battle raged, Lowe went on to tell the remaining Marines in his squad, "Even though they kill one of us, it just makes us come together more; this shows how much we have to stick together. All we have is us."

He further reflected on that moment, which seems forever frozen in his memory: "Once you get the EGA (Eagle, Globe, and Anchor), and been with grunts that have been in combat, you all have something in common. You know the Marine next to you will die for you, and you will die for that Marine; that's the connection that makes you one. We were one."

The battle continued to rage, and 3rd Squad still had work to do. As the squad pushed on to clear the next house, "Natasha," a D9 armored bulldozer on loan from Israel, leveled the building where Hanks died. Natasha was said to be named after an Israeli woman, the wife of an army officer, who was killed by a suicide bomber.

As the platoon watched the destruction of the building, no one said a word. It was instant justice. *"I hope they all get crushed alive. These bastards are all hyped up on drugs; they deserve a painful death,"*

Private Francisco Contreras was thinking. As we pushed further into the city, I found the RPK that killed Hanks in the rubble of the building, along with a red-checkered scarf, universally worn by the jihadis, covered in blood and riddled by bullet holes.

Gunny Hackett and Lieutenant Sommers led 1st Platoon's survivors forward. In the distance, Sommers and I spotted a muj on a rooftop. Sommers looked at Hackett and said, "Let me show you how it's done." Sommers took careful aim with his M16.

With one shot, he killed a sniper over 300 meters away.

"Nice shot," said Hackett.

The platoon moved west and took shelter in the company go firm house, the palace of the Sheikh of Fallujah. The sun set on another horrible day in Fallujah.

15

D9s

We have never taken this operation seriously enough. We have never provided enough troops . . . We have never worked the intelligence part of the war in a serious and sustained fashion.

—A retired senior military official with experience in Iraq, *Time magazine*, September 26, 2005

As NIGHT FELL ON NOVEMBER 17, Lima Company was holed up in the palace of the Sheikh of Fallujah. Surprisingly, despite the full-scale battle raging all around, most of the mayor's furnishings remained intact, even his massive widescreen TV. The men scrounged up every blanket and mat they could find. Most of the mats had a disheveled, slept-on appearance; most likely, they had been used the night before by the enemy. The men fortified the entrances, and crammed themselves into a ten-by-thirty-foot room. To clear space for bedding down, they used a piece of broken wood as a crude broom to sweep out broken glass on the floor.

At night, the temperature plummeted below freezing. The Marines paired off, sleeping back to back under shared blankets to conserve body heat. They slept in a semi-fetal position, uniforms tucked in everywhere possible, hands in their crotches for warmth. They were chilled to the bone.

Shortly after 8:00 p.m., a darkened figure entered the room. "Who the fuck is that?" Every Marine reached for his M16. A second later, someone shouted, "It's okay, it's just a Shwanny." "Shwanny" was the Marine nickname for an Iraqi tribe that provided many men to the Iraqi special forces. In this case, it was most likely a CAP India Iraqi. The Shwanny tore through a box of MREs, already "rat fucked" by the Marines. To "rat fuck" means to pluck out and devour all the goodies in the MREs, like M&Ms and Pop Tarts. Combat saps all your strength and energy, and can lead to rapid weight loss. Everyone's cheekbones seem to grow more pronounced as the battle drags on.

Outside the palace, staccato eruptions of small-arms fire, RPGs, and mortars rocked the night. Dragon Eyes, the tiny, pilotless airplanes that beamed real-time images of the battlefield back to battalion headquarters, constantly buzzed in the background. The most comforting sound in the dark was the chainsaw *brrrrrr, brrrrrr, brrrrrr* of Basher's 25mm Gatling gun. "That's our guardian angel," said one Marine. Using its superior infrared optics, Basher accurately identified enemy fighter near our position and destroyed them. Scores were killed every night slinking through the shadows as they tried to outflank Lima.

Suddenly, the sound of battle was interrupted by an incongruous sound. "*Meow, meow, meow.*" One of the Marines hollered, "What the fuck? Get the fuck out of here."

"It's a cat."

"Leave it alone, it's not hurting anyone." At night, stray cats and dogs patrolled the streets of Fallujah, looking for food. The dogs, nasty, mangy, and junkyard-mean, usually ran in packs and loved to bark at the men. The cats, on the other hand, roamed around in ones and twos, remaining proudly independent.

The cat, a tiny kitten with crossed green eyes, started purring in my ear. The man next to me, Corporal Mike Henning of Alexandria, Virginia, said "What a stress reliever. Animals bring back our humanity. After killing people and seeing people get killed all week, it's the animals that bring it back."

The men considered Henning, thirty-one, to be the "old man" of the group. He joined the Corps at twenty-eight, out of patriotism. Henning said to me, "Sir, today sucked; now you feel how we feel. When you lose a Marine, it's like losing part of yourself. I feel sorry for the children who lost a father over here." Henning lowered his voice. "I want you to do something for me. This is very important to me. If I don't make it home, I want you to tell my mother I love her."

I replied, "You'll make it home. I know you'll make it home."

As they stood in the courtyard of the pockmarked palace of the mayor of Fallujah, Lima Company's officers and NCOs were alert but disheveled, following the long night of attacks by the jihadis. Small-arms fire echoed in the background as heavy black smoke billowed toward the indigo blue sky. It was time for the November 18 daily morning briefing.

Lima Company's thirty-two-year-old commander, Captain Brian Heatherman, issued a new set of orders to his platoon leaders. "We're no longer in the business of clearing houses with Marines. Lay suppressing fire down on the houses and put a rocket in it first. No Marines go into houses without it getting rocketed first. D9s follow." Heatherman had thought about pulling 1st Platoon out of the line, but decided against it, because withdrawing the men would go against everything the Marines had fought for thus far. As a morale booster, he gave 1st Platoon control of two D9 bulldozers to flatten any muj strongpoints encountered during the advance.

Heatherman, a born leader, commanded the respect of every

Marine in his company—not least because he refused to sacrifice any more of his men by minimizing the damage to Fallujah. To hell with political correctness. Heatherman—the entire company, actually—was galvanized by the death of Hanks the previous day. "Some people snapped after Hanks was killed," recalled Conner.

The company had already lost more than seven dead, and nearly 50 percent of the men in the battalion had been wounded. Many of them refused a second Purple Heart, out of respect for the medal and those who have earned it in the past. First Platoon had over 70 percent wounded and four men killed in action, more than any other platoon in the battle. Hanks was the last straw. The consensus was, "No more dead Marines."

About an hour after Captain Heatherman's briefing, 1st Platoon moved up to the jump-off point, a house with a huge walled courtyard near the road designated Phase Line Isabel. First Platoon's mission was to flatten everything in its path over the next mile or so. Days of constant battle had left every Marine tired, dirty, and smelling like shit. "Like a hajji trash dump," one Marine snidely remarked. Still, no one complained.

The Marines entered the courtyard; about six Hummers were parked inside its gray walls. Inside the courtyard, the mood was relaxed, with rap music playing in the background. Three Marines were on the roof firing rockets at buildings in the block Lima was about to destroy.

"Spot!" A Marine fired a spotting round from the top of the two-story house.

"Rocket!" A rocket thundered forward and detonated inside a nearby building, kicking up dust and debris. M1A2 tanks fired rounds into the buildings directly in front of the platoon.

While they waited for the preparatory bombardment to be completed, the men moved from the courtyard into the house to find a place to hunker down. Rosalez flipped over a coffee table to get at a chair buried in the rubble. A weapon wrapped in a sack was strapped to the bottom of the table, an SKS semi-automatic rifle, complete with a shiny new steel bayonet.

The entire city was littered with weapons caches. A favorite muj tactic was to fight dressed in civilian clothes. When things got too hot, they would abandon their weapons and move, unarmed, to another position. The Marines' ROEs forbade firing on unarmed civilians, so the jihadis could move unhindered to another cache, pick up a hidden weapon, and resume fighting. By this stage of the battle, however, the city had effectively become a free-fire zone.

"First Platoon, move out!" The men carefully crept past Phase Line Isabel. Nearly every building was rubble. "This place looks like a Hollywood set," remarked one of the men. Sommers calmly directed his men into position as he puffed on a Korean Pine cigarette. His posture was ramrod straight as he moved around the battlefield, rarely taking cover even in the face of incoming fire.

Over the radio, everyone heard the latest Dragon Eye report: "There's a platoon-sized element of muj maneuvering in your area." Down to fewer than twenty men, 1st Platoon was outnumbered by the jihadis.

A trailer from a flatbed truck provided some cover as the men crept forward across the open road. Avoiding enemy fire, they flattened themselves against a large, grayish cinderblock wall surrounding the first building designated for destruction. Bodek and his combat engineers took the point. "Nice combat glide," one of the infantrymen remarked acidly, as Bodek aimed his M16 like a special operations veteran and moved toward the building. The team slithered around the ten-foot-high outer wall and approached an opening leading to the door of the building. The area around the building was littered with trash and the debris of battle. Spent syringes were lying all over the place.

"Contact!" At least one shadowy figure was lurking in the building like a spider, hoping to kill a Marine with a lucky face shot.

"There's muj inside," barked Bodek. "Stay back from the door!" Bodek charged forward and fired into the open doorway. His assistant, a corporal nicknamed "Jackrabbit," moved into position with a Bangalore torpedo.

"Bangalore up!"

"Bangalore's up."

"Suppressing fire!" More men fired volleys of M16 fire into the doorway as Jackrabbit rested the Bangalore in a small hole in the wall.

"Jackrabbit, light it so we can get the fuck out of here!"

The corporal, who hailed from Lynchburg, Virginia, had the look and accent of a soldier from General Robert E. Lee's Army of Northern Virginia. He was also as brave as any Confederate soldier. He lifted the torpedo up to a hole in the wall above his head, lit the fuse, and shoved the Bangalore into the house.

"Fire in the hole!"

"Go!"

"Go!"

The men charged like mad back to the tractor trailer. The house exploded, leaving a pile of rubble and a plume of dust.

"Hey, there's someone behind that courtyard wall."

"I've got just the trick for that," said Bodek. The combat engineer hustled forward with a claymore mine attached to a broomstick. Used extensively in Vietnam, the claymore contains scores of metal BBs that spray outward, killing or wounding anyone in their path. Bodek extended the mine over the wall.

"Fire in the hole!"

Simultaneously, the jihadis in the courtyard hurled grenades over the wall.

The claymore and grenades detonated at the same time. The BBs shredded the enemy fighters inside the courtyard, but at least one BB flew back down the broomstick and hit Bodek in the hand. Bleeding, he bandaged it up and pushed forward. He looked over at me and said, "You have brass balls for being out here with us." After the battle, a surgeon removed the BB and several fragments from the insurgent's grenades. Bodek received the Purple Heart his father-in-law had admonished him not to earn.

Natasha, one of the D9 bulldozers, rumbled forward and pulverized the courtyard and building. Most of the block was scheduled to either be blown up by demolitions or flattened by a dozer.

"What's the difference between a building being bulldozed and bombed?"

"Nothing," replied Sergeant Kyle, as the platoon pushed forward.

Only Sojda, Wade, Garza, Turpen, Alavez, Lowe, and Contreras were left from 3rd Squad. They took the lead as the platoon drove farther south into Queens. The terrain started opening up, and 3rd Squad skirted the side of Isaac Field, a large open area in front of the platoon's advance.

Meanwhile, 2nd Platoon, several hundred yards to the right, reported over the radio that they found an enemy field hospital, a house filled with a cache of medical supplies. Many of the boxes in the house were labeled "World Health Organization." Several bloody mats apparently had been used as makeshift litters for wounded jihadis. A half-eaten bowl of rice lay in a corner, beside a pile of filthy pots and pans.

The battalion commander, Lieutenant Colonel Willie Buhl, arrived on the scene to inspect the field hospital. Several Iraqi Special Special Forces (SSF) soldiers, including a warrant officer named Majid, were holding the house.

Buhl approached Majid to say, "It doesn't happen enough, but I want to thank you for your service here." Buhl shook the Iraqi warrant officer's hand, and presented each Iraqi soldier with the Marine Eagle, Globe, and Anchor. The Iraqis beamed with pride.

Meanwhile, the battalion intelligence officer took pictures of the boxes of medical supplies. Minutes passed, and Buhl's entourage moved outside, just in time for a firefight.

"There's a motherfucker!" screamed a 2nd Platoon Marine. A muj had been spotted moving into the building next to the field hospital. The figure was so close that when he moved through the courtyard next to the aid station, his body briefly blocked the light coming through the gaps in the courtyard wall. The squad tasked with clearing the house was suspicious, because the windows and doors were covered with boards and blankets; they were unaware of the figure moving into the building. "The place just didn't look right, we all had a weird feeling about it," recalled Lance Corporal Brenden Wright, who was pulling security outside the house for the breach team.

After a Marine kicked in the front door, Majid followed the squad into the building. The first room was clear. Majid and Lance Corporal Louis Figueroa advanced to the next interior door. "Fig" Figueroa was a popular figure in 2nd Platoon. He came from a tough background in a Los Angeles barrio, and like many of his fellow Marines, was taking advantage of the new life offered by the Corps.

Figueroa expected Majid to stack behind the door and wait for him to open it. Instead, Majid opened the door himself, revealing an RPK team waiting in ambush. A hailstorm of bullets flew into the fatal funnel, knocking down Majid and Figueroa. Lance Corporal Luis Martinez and another Shwanny emptied their magazines into the room, hitting one muj in the face and a second in the chest. According to Martinez, he was yelling "Corpsman up!" when several other Shwannies "freaked out and grabbed Majid," and carried him out of the building.

Second Platoon's squad tumbled out of the building as well, shouting "Fig's down, Fig's down!" Staff Sergeant Van Daele ordered Corpsman Elliot Yoshimura to "go back in there with Martinez and bring Fig out." As Yoshimura and Martinez moved past Majid, the courageous Iraqi, despite a sucking chest wound and a gaping hole in his neck, gasped a final warning: "Mujahideen. Mujahideen."

Martinez, several other Marines, and Yoshimura carefully reentered the house. Yoshimura recalled what happened next. "I ran up into the room and saw a lot of movement, and threw in a frag. I found Fig's SAW, which was all torn up. I went through the door where Fig went down, grabbed the handle of his assault vest, and dragged his body out. We saw more movement, and threw another frag."

As Marines and Shwannies carried Fig and Majid into the courtyard of the muj field hospital, a Marine assaultman demolished the house with a satchel charge.

In the courtyard, corpsmen feverishly worked on the men with forceps, but too much damage had been done. Ironically, a three-foot-high box of brand new Korans lay next to the fallen men. Religious fanaticism was the fuel of the jihadi effort.

The clank and whine of Abrams main battle tanks resounded in the distance. Two tanks moved into position and blasted the entire area in front of the battalion, while artillery fire rained down south of the courtyard.

"A symphony of fire," observed Buhl, quoting General George Patton's term describing combined arms. The block was suppressed, its buildings reduced to rubble.

Like Hanks before him, Fig was killed by international terrorists, as the battalion's Command Chronology established: "Once the enemy's defense was broken as the Battalion penetrated and began to employ combined arms within its own battle space, the enemy elected to wait and engage Marines from inside structures at very close range. The caliber of the enemy proficiency also significantly improved as the Battalion advanced south. It is believed that the fanatical international terrorists encountered to the south were, for the most part, better trained and more determined to resist to the death against their Marine adversaries."

The terrorists were remarkably disciplined, for people who considered themselves walking dead men. Sommers was impressed with them: "knowing that you're about to die, but still able to wait for the last two inches of the door to open up before pulling the trigger, just to have the chance to take one or two Americans out with you before you go."

Back in 1st Platoon's sector, the combat engineers continued to clear the area by blowing house after house in succession. There is a thrill in destruction. With Hanks, Larson, Wood, and Bryan on everyone's minds, payback and survival became intertwined.

Halfway down the block, Natasha broke down. The constant wear and tear of fighting in the city finally took its toll. Luckily, resistance was light.

Sojda and Bodek discovered a massive underground bunker bursting with weapons: mortar tubes, 155mm rounds made into IEDs, scores of different sized mortar rounds, and two anti-aircraft guns pointing the wrong way. "We found anti-aircraft guns oriented south. It was our first indication that their defenses were planned for an attack from the south," recalled Sommers.

Throughout Queens, fighting positions and IEDs were prepared to defend toward the south. The American campaign of raids, feints, and disinformation, intended to deceive the defenders about the direction of the main assault, had been a success.

As 3rd Squad probed around outside the bunker, they found a dead suicide bomber in a fighting hole. He was wearing a vest filled with explosives, the detonation trigger dangling from his outstretched hand. The suicide bomber is perhaps the ultimate expression of the jihadi culture of death. "They don't subscribe to any sort of moral law," said Sommers.

Rosalez turned the enemy's weapons against him and also removed a threat from the battlefield. "I had the honor of putting one of the 155mm IEDs found in the bunker on the suicide bomber. I snipped the wires and placed it on the body and blew it up in place."

Night was falling rapidly, and Lima had to scramble to find a house to go firm before darkness fell. The company wound up in another large mansion. Fighting around the house was lighter that night, but still active.

In the house, conversation turned to the meaning of the battle.

"We've sure killed a lot of terrorists."

"I wonder if we created new ones, when we destroyed this city," someone murmured.

The point might have been valid if Fallujah had been defended by a genuine, home-grown insurgency, but such was not the case. A month of intelligence work would reveal that the bulk of the jihadi forces defending Fallujah came from outside Iraq. Most of the so-called "insurgents" were carrying the same version of an Iraqi ID card. The facility manufacturing the cards was later discovered by 3/1, and documents found at the site revealed that the jihadis came from 18 different countries. The Marines found rosters of entire companies of Syrian and Saudi volunteers, and evidence of a large presence of al-Qaeda members. Iraq is clearly just one front in a greater, worldwide war.

On the morning of November 19, the men were wakened at 5:30 a.m. As the sun began to pour through the glassless windows, a rumor spread around the second floor of the mansion.

"Lima is retrograding out of the city."

"I don't believe it."

Sommers confirmed the rumor. "We are going back this morning."

Sommers savored the bittersweet moment, "On the plus side, we had finished our part of the attack on a high note: that last day had no serious casualties and we found a cache as well. But we still wanted to go all the way through the city. Our platoon had done the security for the breach over the train tracks to start the whole thing, and by now we felt like we deserved to see the desert on the other side. Marines hate to be taken out of a fight, and this was no different."

The men scrambled to load their gear into the tracks, and piled into the AAVs and Humvees. The vehicles were soon snaking their way through shattered streets back to the grain mill, a largely windowless, pockmarked building. As the drivers navigated around the rubble, someone yelled to me, "Happy Birthday, Pat." I was thinking, *"It's no longer a birthday, it's an 'alive' day."*

Eleven days after the initial assault, Lima Company was being taken off the line and out of the battle for good. Having been among the first to advance into the city, 1st Platoon was among the last to leave.

16

Rest

In the battle for Fallujah, the terrorists hid weapons in a
cemetery. They hid ammunition in private homes.
They hid bombs in mosques, but they could not hide
from the United States Marines.

—*President George W. Bush*

A BULLET-SCARRED IRAQI FLAG FLUTTERED DEFIANTLY ON
the roof of Fallujah's grain mill. The flag did not last long.
Within an hour of their arrival, the Marines of Lima Company
hauled it down and started converting the building into their new
forward operating base.

First Platoon set to work clearing rubble and setting up
makeshift beds behind bags of grain and milling machines. Explosions shook the drab concrete walls of the mill as Bodek and Rosalez blew up most of the nearby houses, to make it harder for any
remaining pockets of jihadis to ambush the company. After surviving America's toughest urban battle since Hue City, the Marines
felt secure within the solid concrete walls of the factory.

Once the platoon carved out a living area within the mill, the
brothers of 3rd Squad climbed to the top floor of the mill and gazed

out at a city in ruins. Over half of Fallujah's 39,000 buildings and homes had been destroyed. Zarqawi and his al-Qaeda terrorists, the jihadis from across the Muslim world, the Sunni insurgents, and the Saddam holdovers, could no longer use Fallujah as a sanctuary. While Zarqawi was still at large, the fight for Fallujah had removed thousands of terrorists from battlefields of Iraq. The cost of clearing the largest terrorist bastion in Iraq had been high: seventy Americans dead, twenty-two of them in 3/1 alone. Nearly half of the men in the battalion would receive the Purple Heart. First Platoon went into the city with forty-five Marines. Fewer than twenty remained. Third Squad was decimated. Sojda lost Hanks, Garza lost Larson, Wade lost Wood, and Stokes lost Bryan. Conner was in the hospital.*

Many of the Marines were wondering, "Why did I survive and my best friend didn't?" Garza told Lance Corporal Derick Lowe, "I don't know why or how I made it through that house [where Larson and Wood were killed] alive. I swear to God, those bullets were whizzing by my face. I felt like I had a guardian around me. I don't know how I didn't get hit; I can still hear the bullets whizzing by my ear."

*The Thundering Third accounted for the largest number of confirmed enemy kills, approximately one thousand (1st Platoon alone killed at least sixty-one fighters, 6 percent of the total). During the battle, 3/1 also captured 1,200 enemy fighters. Strikingly, half of the total 2,500 muj captured during the battle of Fallujah were released within seventy-two hours, thanks largely to detention rules that demanded, among other things, two signed affidavits from coalition or Iraqi forces that a recently captured prisoner was a combatant. Naturally, in the chaos of urban warfare, there was not sufficient time or manpower to complete most of the formal paperwork. Many prisoners were set free simply because they kept their mouths shut, or because there was a "lack of evidence" to hold them. This broken detention policy continues to have a devastating impact on the safety of our troops and the Iraqi people.

The men chose places along the walls to put their gear and unroll their sleeping bags. It should have been their first decent night's sleep in weeks, but for many, their rest was stolen by nightmares. In his dreams, Garza met his best friend again. "I dreamed about being at the barracks with Larson and we were together on leave. We all came home and then I woke up. I still think about them, all of the guys we lost. There's nothing I can do."

Every night, while stationed in Iraq, Sojda relived the deaths of Bryan and Hanks. "The exact same dream replayed over and over again."

The battle was also replaying in Sergeant Conner's mind. After being hit in the arm three times on November 17th, he was medevaced from Fallujah to a series of field hospitals in Iraq, and finally to a hospital in Germany. The first part of his journey included an unexpected bedfellow. "They put me in an ambulance on the way to the LZ [landing zone] with a guy who was all banged up and an enemy prisoner of war. I was able to sit up and I looked over at the EPW. I don't know if he was stoned out of his mind, or he was really scared, he just lay there with his eyes open. He didn't blink, didn't move, or anything. The other soldier I was with was really messed up and kept saying, 'This sucks, I can't believe they put one of them in here with us.' I ignored it. I just kept wondering where I was going and kept replaying what happened over the past week."

After riding in a medical transport plane that looked and sounded like "a Civil War field hospital," Conner made it safely to the Landstuhl Regional Medical Center in Germany, the biggest American hospital outside the United States. After three operations, the doctors managed to remove Conner's shrapnel and bullet fragments.

In the hospital, Conner ran into Huyett. The two Marines reminisced about the battle and discussed their plans once they returned to the States. On their last day in Germany, the two Marine brothers received care packages delivered randomly to American troops overseas. Conner's package included a hand-crocheted American flag. It became one of his prized possessions, and he wrapped himself in it during the long flight home.

By November 21, major combat operations officially ceased in the city. A new phase of the Fallujah operation replaced house clearing—Security and Stabilization Operations (SASO) patrols were implemented to pave the way for civilians to reenter the city. Privately, most of the platoon wondered how civilians could return to the city with pockets of jihadis still lurking around. Letting civilians in also could allow more muj back into the city.

Nevertheless, the Marines kept a tight lip and started patrolling a fairly large area of operations on the western edge of the city. The bridge where the Blackwater contractors were killed was the platoon's northern border, with the territory extending about half a mile south of the major bridge over the Euphrates. Pockets of jihadis were still cropping up here and there. The tension of clearing rooms did not go away. "You still don't know if anything is going to happen. It's not 100 percent clear. Every day we were there, that tension was replaying in our heads," recalled Sojda.

After being blasted by a Chechen grenade, Private Stokes recovered from his wounds and returned to the platoon. While clearing houses on a routine SASO patrol, the twenty-one-year-old private tripped over a jihadi hiding under a blanket. The hand-to-hand fight ended with Stokes killing the man with a trench knife. It was Stokes's ninth kill in the city.

In another incident, the platoon discovered a resourceful insurgent holed up in a house. According to Lieutenant Sommers, "We were on patrol, standard back clearing. We got up to one house, went in, and heard someone upstairs. No problem, blow up the house. We exit the house and ready a Bangalore torpedo. Detonation in 30 seconds! Nothing happens. We wait another minute, nothing. We go back inside. The guy had come down the stairs, pulled the blasting cap off the explosive, and gone back upstairs. We were pissed, so we redid it with a shorter fuse and fired lots of SMAW rounds into the house at the same time. The house blew up."

After locating a vast quantity of unexploded ordnance and re-clearing thousands of rooms, most of them empty, Lima Company was rotated back to Camp Fallujah for a few hours of R&R, and their first hot showers in weeks. After living in the field for three weeks, the Marines were quite ripe. When they arrived at the camp, a hot Thanksgiving turkey dinner with all the trimmings was waiting for them. While moving through the chow line, Sojda ran into a high-ranking officer who asked him if he was wounded during the battle. With a stone-cold expression he responded, "Sir, everybody, in my opinion, was wounded; whether you shed blood or not, your memories are scarred for life."

"That's a good way of putting it," the officer responded glumly.

Despite everyone's wounds, the meal was a tremendous morale booster. "I know my heart went back into the right spot. It was down to my feet. The entire platoon sat together. It was the best dinner I ever had, my first hot meal in nearly a month," recalled Sojda.

According to Lieutenant Sommers, "I think I ate more than I had any other Thanksgiving. Bacon cheeseburgers rule! Showers felt great. The area outside Fallujah, which a month earlier made us nervous, now seemed like a vacation spot." Sommers got on the Internet to see what had happened in the world during the past three weeks, and was relieved to find an email from his best friend, who had also been fighting in Fallujah. "We also got our beer/rum ration from the USMC birthday when we went back. So we just sat around smoking, playing dice, playing Risk, drinking beer, and everyone just put the battle behind them."

Thanksgiving at Camp Fallujah wasn't all beer and skittles; the men began to face the cold reality of the loss of their friends. According to Sojda, "Thanksgiving, an American tradition, I think that's when everybody felt it hit home that not everybody is coming back. I couldn't help but think about Mikey [Hanks] and the other guys who were killed, who weren't going to eat Thanksgiving dinner. This was the first holiday they missed."

With hot turkey in their bellies, nobody complained when the platoon returned to the city and resumed patrolling. The monotony was broken up by lighter moments, as Sommers recalls. "After that meal we were feeling pretty good and we were doing back clearing, standard stuff. Before we entered a room, we threw a grenade, just to be on the safe side. All the rubble creates spider holes, and spaces where someone could hide, so we'd throw a grenade down there. Then Lowe throws a grenade into a hole in a driveway. I've heard a lot of grenades explode and they are usually loud, but this one just made a dull thud, and all of a sudden this black rain starts coming down. I'm covered in Iraqi excrement, just covered in it. Everyone had a good time with that."

First Platoon's SASO patrols would continue through November into January. The Thundering Third was scheduled to go home before the Iraqi elections at the end of January. The elections represented another turning point in the war in Iraq: for the first time, the people of Iraq would have an opportunity to participate in their own government.

Just before the New Year, the company received an opportunity to send one Marine home early to his family. All the platoon sergeants were asked to make a case for one of their men. According to

Gunny Hackett, "When it came to me, I said Garza; he lost everybody in his fire team. Everyone in his fire team is gone; he's the only one left. There was silence for a second. Then everyone looked at me and unanimously said, 'He needs to go home. He's the one. Forget about the name I gave you, this Marine needs to go home.'" Garza went home early. The squad kept their blood oath; Garza made it home alive.

During the final two weeks in January, the battalion slowly phased out its operations in Fallujah. Civilians reentered the city. Lima was chosen as one of Fallujah's gatekeepers, because the company had one of the best track records with the Iraqis before the battle. The reception, though, was lukewarm at best. "Most of the people gave us dirty looks or they wouldn't look at you. We just got all the bad guys out of their city; they're safer now, but they didn't seem to care," recalled Sojda.

Most of 1st Platoon returned to the compound outside the main gate of Camp Abu Ghraib. The men performed their routine duties. Everyone seemed to be on autopilot. Eat, sleep, fire watch, and take an occasional shower here and there. The men spent a good deal of time thinking about going home and reflecting on what they had gone through.

Many men tried to find meaning in the battle. Rosalez explained why they fought: "It was about the man to your left and right. We don't do this for freedom, apple pie, but for the man to the left and right. The privates, lance corporals, and sergeants stand shoulder-to-shoulder in the face of the enemy, the honor among men.

"We grew into a brotherhood. What we had was completely free and clear, there was no race, no bills that had to be paid. It wasn't about money; that was all gone. We worked side-by-side to destroy the enemy who was trying to destroy us."

Conner, back in the U.S. after multiple surgeries, was also reflecting on the battle. His family realized he had gone through hell and did not press him to talk about it. Only combat veterans understood. When Conner went to a VA hospital to get the staples in his arm removed, a Vietnam veteran in a wheelchair approached him.

"Semper Fi," the veteran said to Conner. "The vet knew most of the men in the ward; they were not combat veterans. All these guys wish they could be us. They weren't in it. They don't understand." There's something only combat veterans who were "in the shit" fully appreciate.

Back at Camp Abu Ghraib, the battalion packed their gear. A few days before their departure, the men were assembled on the grinder. Colonel Mike Shupp praised the entire Thundering Third for their service in Iraq and bid them farewell.

"I don't think there is anyone in the Marine Corps that could do what you have done today. I can't tell you how proud I am of you. How proud the whole regiment is of your service. It is bittersweet that we see you going home. Let me tell you again, you have made the nation, the Marine Corps, and everyone proud of your service. No one will forget. I know you won't. I don't think any of us will.

"It has been a great fight we have had together taking Fallujah. You did it. Some people thought it would never get done. You went in and achieved it. Magnificent battle. You did it like real pros. You did it because of each other.

"You are ready to go home now. I want you to keep your guard up. You made it through as buddies, friends, Marines. I want you to look out for each other all the way back home. I want you to make sure you take care of each other, till you get off that plane and into the arms of your loved ones. And then when you get home, I want you to have a hell of a good time. I want you to just kick back and raise some hell. I want you to enjoy it—you earned it. Make sure you enjoy it with your family, friends, and loved ones.

"A lot of people talk about the Greatest Generation. It was after World War II that they became the Greatest Generation, leaders of our country, because they went through the same things that you have gone through on the battlefields out here in Iraq. They understand what the sacrifice for freedom is all about. They had an inner confidence in themselves that they could do anything. You are the Greatest Generation. Your experience has paved the way for the future. I expect to see you as the future leaders of the Marine Corps. I expect to see you as leaders of business, leaders of our country. You are the Greatest Generation. With the experiences you have gained here, you can do anything if you set your mind to it. Never forget."

17

Requiem

Before they returned to the united states, lima Company went through one more ceremony. The Marines reverently filed into Camp Abu Ghraib's mess hall, silently moving through a set of double doors. Written above the door frame in flat black paint was "Gone, But Not Forgotten," and the names of the fallen who perished in Fallujah. Troopers from the 82nd Airborne, who occupied the camp before the Marines, made up most of the list. Eventually, the Marines added their fallen comrades to the wall. January 20, 2005, was a day of closure, a day to celebrate, to never forget, seven Lima warriors.

At the front of the room the weapons of the fallen stood upright. Their helmets were carefully placed on the stock of each fallen Marine's weapon, and their boots rested at the base. Seven rough crosses symbolically represented each fallen Marine. The survivors of Lima Company silently passed by the crosses and formed into platoons by rank. In a commanding voice, Gunny Wilson took the roll. As their names were called, Marine after Marine stood up and responded, "Here, Gunnery Sergeant." Then Wilson came to the name of the first fallen man.

"Lance Corporal Bryan." Silence.

"Lance Corporal Benjamin Bryan." Silence.

"Lance Corporal Benjamin S. Bryan."

Wilson resumed calling out the names on the roster. Eventually, all seven fallen Marines were called.

The chaplain spoke briefly to begin the ceremony, and turned over the podium to the surviving Marines, who spoke about their fallen best friends. They spoke from the heart, and delivered beautiful tributes to their friends. The Marines in the audience fought back tears. Sojda was the first Marine from 1st Platoon to speak and honor his best friend, Lance Corporal Michael Hanks.

"Today is the day we honor and mourn our fallen heroes of Lima Company. Our brothers who fought beside us through thick and thin, who made the ultimate sacrifice, not for God, not for country, not for the Corps, but for the friends who fought beside them. Lance Corporal Michael Hanks was one of them. Everyone in the battalion knew him. He inspired everybody with his stories and actions. He was a friend to many, and anyone who knew him knew he would give the shirt off his back or his last dollar to anyone who asked. He was funny, brave, smart, and a hero.

"He always talked about going home, partying, now that he had his new friends. Mikey loved to talk, even if nobody was listening. He would talk and talk. I caught him one time in a room by himself, just talking. I asked him, 'Hey man, what are you doing?' He said, 'Just listening to myself talk.' He loved his family, his friends; he talked about them often, to the point that I knew them myself.

"On the other hand, if he didn't like you, you knew it. He always had choice words for people he didn't like. He wasn't afraid to let them know it.

"Mikey always wanted to take point on patrols, be it in training at Pendleton or fighting in the city of Fallujah. It was nearly impossible to persuade him to bring up the rear. He would always say, 'Up front is where the action is.' He was a fiend for action. Mikey was a warrior, and he died as a warrior. He wouldn't have it any other way. I know he is looking down right now protecting us, just like he would if we were here. Mike, now your friends at Lima Company give you a warrior's funeral. You will remain in our hearts for eternity and you will never be forgotten."

Stokes spoke about Bryan. "We come together today to remember our fallen brothers and fellow Lima warrior, Lance Corporal Benjamin Bryan. He was a friend to many, a son, someone who will never be forgotten by those of us who knew him. Bryan didn't have visions of grandeur; he wanted to drive a Budweiser truck. He wanted to live in the freedom he helped protect. Bryan wasn't the loudest, he didn't have the best uniform, but he was always prepared. He would never back down in the face of danger. He was always Semper Fi. He was a Carolina Panthers fan. He loved Xbox and was great at Halo, and eager to get home to master Halo II and beat everybody in the barracks. He was the kind of guy who would always give away his last dip, his last cigarette, last drink of his soda. Bryan was just another one of America's sons who loved his country and paid the highest price when he was called upon. He was never outspoken, he was truly sensitive. You could always count on him, because the last thing he wanted was to let his buddies down. Bryan, if you are listening, I will always use my memories of you as an inspiration in my life. Life is too short, too fragile to waste. As we remember the last ten months, we accomplished our mission in Fallujah due to your sacrifice and all of our brothers that we lost. I will never forget you and look forward to seeing you in the next life."

Lowe spoke about his close friend, Nicholas Larson. "We come here today to remember fellow warriors who did not make it through the battle, one of them being my friend Nicholas Larson. He was a friend of many, a Marine who could get the job done; he was a soon-to-be loving husband. Larson was a person you could go to when you were feeling down, when you needed a laugh or just to have fun.

"Larson also loved to work out. I remember when we had to get ready to go on patrol in thirty minutes, he would always want to work out real quick. I would always say, 'We have to go in thirty minutes.' He would respond, 'Even better, I'll feel it.'

"Larson was eager to get married when he got home from this deployment. He would always talk to me about having a kid, starting a family. He always wanted a home to come home to, after he got off work, so he could spend time with his kid and new wife.

"Larson is gone now and all we have are memories. He would not want us to mourn his death, but would want us to remember the good times we had, times that weren't so good that we made good together. He'd want us to be proud of what we finished all together on the morning of November 9th. Larson, you will not be forgotten, brother; we will remember you for the rest of our lives. We all know that we have you up above as an overwatch, for the rest our time on earth, until we are up there with you. Rest in peace, Larson."

Steven Wade was the last 3rd Squad Marine to speak. He spoke with conviction about his best friend, Nathan Wood. "Today we are here to commemorate our fellow brothers, and Lance Corporal Nathan Wood, a good friend to me and a good Marine.

"For the Marines who went before him, he was courageous and nice, a perfect all-around Marine. It's times like these when our country calls us to war; infantry Marines like us are ready.

"Nat was a tough guy, but was never one to talk about his experiences. But those of us in the platoon, every time we saw Nat, we knew he had something to say. He would always talk about the plans he had, how he and his family had trips planned when he got out. The bar he and his friends would like to open up.

"The times I remember are when we got off work and we'd order a pizza, watch movies, and have a good time. But for those of us who knew him, we know that he wouldn't want us to dwell on his death, but keep going, and keep on going. Rest in peace, brother."

After the last eulogy, Captain Heatherman addressed his company. "It's been a long few months and we've done a lot in that time. You know, as Marines, we do it all—whether it be working humanitarian assistance sites, or training the Iraqi Army how to secure their own country. I don't need to tell remind you that when the call came, we did what Marines do best—destroy the enemy. These men, these fine Marines, Lima warriors, died doing what they love. Doing what they were born to do: defeat a determined enemy. We can probably find comfort in the fact we destroyed the insurgents who actually killed our brothers; I know I sure will.

"But think about this. It's been said the best revenge is living well. I think we should all live well for our brothers who have fallen. This disillusioned enemy that you faced and destroyed will never know the life he could have had, the life we will enjoy in the United States—the life that our fallen brothers loved, lived for, and want to see you carry on. Live your lives well for the men who fought alongside us.

"I imagine the path to heaven is clear now. I'm pretty sure, I have a sneaking suspicion that in true warrior fashion, that they could have stacked up at the gates of heaven, they could have lifted the gate off its hinges. Lance Corporal Hanks is probably there with a field-expedient Bangalore. Sergeant Calderon, Sergeant James,

Hanks, Wood, Fig, Bowling, Bryan, and Larson, live well, and never forget."

After Heatherman's speech, each Marine paid his personal respects to his fallen comrades. Most took a knee in front of the Marine they were closest to and silently prayed.

18

Home

A DAY BEFORE DEPARTING FROM IRAQ DURING THE THIRD week of January 2005, the Marines gathered back at the mess hall and completed the paperwork that cleared the path to return to the U.S. They were also urged to attend a post-traumatic stress disorder (PTSD) class.

The hour-long class covered the basics of PTSD. The battalion had gone through urban warfare, the toughest, most personal combat an infantryman can endure. Most of the Marines were wondering whether they suffered from PTSD already, or would it affect them when they returned to the States? One senior officer at the meeting bluntly stated, "If you were back in the States and normal Americans endured what you went through in Fallujah, they would be holding group therapy and all-night candle vigils." The Marines were expected to be tougher than the average American.

Everyone was coping with the memories of the battle in his own way. Most buried their feelings about the battle. "I wonder if I should talk to a shrink, but I don't want to hurt my career," remarked one Marine. No one complained openly about what they endured in Fallujah and everyone was proud of his role in the battle, but many of the men privately thought the class whitewashed PTSD. "They gave us the same exact class we got when you return from a normal deployment in Hawaii or Australia. It was my third deployment; I thought the class was bullshit. What we went through was different. Granted, not everybody was fucked up in the head, but what percentage was going to seek help? Not many. They should have nipped it in the bud earlier."

Another Marine, concerned about the long term effects of the battle on his men, stated, "All they've done is put their lives on the line. They should not be treated as just another Marine trigger-puller. They have lives, and many of their minds are fucked up. I'm not saying pull them out of the fight, just sit down and talk to them. Find out what they are experiencing. The way the system works, it's a secret to everybody. You don't want to tell anybody because you don't want anyone to think you are a pussy." Some Marines looked at the experience in a more positive light: "what doesn't kill you makes you stronger."

The experience made many of the veterans of Fallujah realize the importance of enjoying life, relationships, and the simple things most people take for granted. For them, the touchy-feely stuff was pushed to the side, at least in the short term, and they focused on coming home.

On January 21, Lima Company's long line of seven-ton trucks pulled out of Camp Abu Ghraib's main gate under the cover of darkness. The convoy's destination was al-Taqaddum Air Base (TQ), the main Marine airhead in Iraq, and the first leg of the journey to Kuwait and home. Lima Company took a long, two-hour-plus circular route around Fallujah to avoid IEDs and ambushes. Losing a Marine who survived the battle and was now on his way home would be unthinkable. Luckily, tragedy did not strike. The entire battalion made it to TQ safely, and the men spent several days in tents waiting for a flight to Kuwait.

The night before he flew to Kuwait, Wade summed up his feelings: "This has been a long-awaited departure. But you feel like you are leaving somebody behind over here. I wouldn't want this to be nobody's soul's last resting place. Not this hell hole. I'm glad we are departing."

At Kuwait International Airport, as the men prepared to board a commercial airliner taking them home, someone barked, "No group pictures until we get on the plane." No one in 3rd Squad was taking any chances.

Everyone in the squad was carrying his own weapon, an M16, SAW, or 203. Many Marines had two weapons, their own and that of a critically wounded or fallen Marine. Lance Corporal Benjamin Hudson was carrying Michael Hanks's battle-scarred 203. In spirit, the fallen Marines were coming home with their brothers.

The flight home was glorious. The Marines traded places with the airline stewardesses and served their fellow Marines soft drinks. The flight's first stop was Shannon International Airport in Ireland, where the airport pubs stayed open to accommodate the thirsty Marines.

No one slept during the long flight home. When the pilot announced the plane had entered U.S. airspace, the Marines let out a massive cheer and clapped their hands. It was an electric moment. The plane touched down in Bangor, Maine, for refueling. Waiting in the airport lobby to greet the Marines, as they do every returning plane of veterans from Iraq or Afghanistan, were scores of Bangor-area World War II, Korea, and Vietnam veterans. Banners proclaimed "Welcome Home." The Bangor veterans, sporting patches, pins and hats from their own wars, greeted each Marine with a firm handshake and a warm smile. A tearful Swift Boat vet said, "I'm doing this because, when we returned from Nam, nobody shook my hand. I don't want that to ever happen to another combat veteran."

After refueling, the plane headed to the West Coast, and landed at March Air Force Base. The returning heroes boarded buses and drove through the winding California hills to 3/1's compound in Camp Pendleton.

Scrambling off the bus, the Marines were greeted by cheering and clapping comrades, friends, and family. Conner greeted Sommers with a huge bear hug.

Also present were 3/1 veterans from WWII, Korea, and Vietnam, including the Korea veterans from G Company who had presented the battalion with their battle guidon before the Thundering Third left for Iraq. The veterans of the greatest generation praised the Marines.

Another survivor of the Chosin Reservoir said, "They say our generation set the bar. I think the bar has been moved. I really think this fight required discipline, commitment, and valor beyond what we had been required to fill. They have the indomitable spirit of the Marine grunt. My feeling is that they really are the cream of the crop. We need to look to them for leadership in the future; they really do value, honor, duty, and country."

The day after Labor Day 2005, a little more than seven months after 1st Platoon came home from Fallujah, the Marines boarded a flight headed back to Iraq. Only their families and 3/1's WWII and Korea veterans were there to see them off. For many of the men, it was their third combat tour of duty in Iraq. After the fall of Fallujah, their new area of operation, the Syrian border, had become one of the hotter combat zones in Iraq. There, the men were to face the same international terrorists they defeated in Fallujah.

For the first time in recent memory, when a company came off leave and reported for duty, every single man returned. No one failed to report for duty and no one failed the mandatory drug tests. Deliberately failing a drug test is a convenient way out for anyone who wanted to avoid returning to the war. The men returned together. After surviving Fallujah, the return to Iraq evoked feelings of apprehension and foreboding, but the men were prepared, and they had one another.

Afterword

Why I Went to Iraq and Wrote This Book

ON A SUNNY DAY IN JANUARY 2005, MORE THAN A DOZEN graying WWII, Korea, and Vietnam veterans were standing shoulder to shoulder outside the barracks at Camp Pendleton, California. Most were clad in red and gold, the distinctive colors of the Marine Corps. All had served in one of the most storied units in the Corps: 3rd Battalion, 1st Marine Regiment, nicknamed the "Thundering Third." Collectively, the men carried the memories of epic Marine Corps battles from Guadalcanal to Korea's Chosin Reservoir to Hue City, Vietnam. The vets had come to Camp Pendleton, the principal Marine base on the West Coast, to welcome home the current incarnation of 3/1 from the battle of Fallujah.

"Look how that tall lieutenant embraces that sergeant, that's an intangible spirit," said one retired colonel, who distinguished himself at the Frozen Chosin. "This is the next greatest generation. I've been a Marine 65 years, been through twelve major campaigns, three and a half wars, I've seen men come and go. The veterans who fought this desert war will be leading the Marine Corps in future years. They are the best of the best, no question." It was the third time I'd heard that intriguing phrase, the next "Greatest Generation."

3/1's homecoming was also my homecoming from Iraq, and the end of a journey that began by happenstance at a veterans' reunion in April 2004. The Static Line Awards Reunion is a huge gathering of airborne veterans and special operators from all of America's wars from WWII to Iraq and Afghanistan. As a guest speaker, I was seated at the main table. To my right sat a highly accomplished paratrooper, a veteran of Vietnam and Iraq, who had just returned from the battlefield. One Command Sergeant Major told me, "I've been coming to these things for the past 20 years and the WWII guys are amazing, but this generation is the next Greatest Generation. What our guys are doing out there is incredible. Privates stepping up the plate doing the job of sergeants. . ."

The Command observation echoed the views of my former neighbor, Colonel Jay Chambers, a regimental commander in the U.S. Army, who also told me, "This is the next greatest generation. Look at what they've done in the past few years in Iraq and Afghanistan with minimal numbers and equipment. Many people at the higher levels never thought they could do it. They thought this was the Nintendo Generation. Some questioned if they'd fight." Chambers's and England's comments made me want to find out just what made the new generation of American soldiers and Marines the next greatest generation.

A month or two after the reunion, I was interviewed on NPR's Diane Rehm Show about my book on America's clandestine WWII agents, *Operatives, Spies, and Saboteurs*. While answering questions from listeners, I was shocked by the NPR audience's lack of understanding of what our troops are doing in Iraq. Some of the comments about Iraq seemed degrading to our troops and the war.

The experience upset me and made me realize I didn't know enough about the war in Iraq either. I wanted to do something, and in some small way, out of patriotism, make a difference.

I noticed nobody seemed to be telling the story of what our troops were doing in the field. The newspapers and broadcast media were focusing almost exclusively on the casualties inflicted by the latest roadside bomb, ignoring the sterling performance of our men in battle, and also their progress in rebuilding Iraq. Most troops were reluctant to talk about their experiences, in part because the wounds were still raw, and also because they were uncomfortable discussing the war with people who hadn't gone through what they had endured. I felt a force driving me to go to Iraq, to experience firsthand what the soldiers were experiencing and help record their stories.

After writing several emails, I obtained permission from CENT-COM (U.S. Central Command) and the Pentagon Public Affairs Office to cover the 509th Parachute, a unit which specializes in acting as the OPFOR (opposing force) in guerrilla warfare training exercises at Fort Polk, Louisiana. More to the point, at least for me, part of the 509th was under orders to fight in Iraq.

However, I couldn't accompany the 509th to the battlefield without the permission of the unit's commanding officer. "Before you go to Iraq," LTC Daniel Griffith told me, "you need to see what we do at Polk." In order to cover the 509th, who consider themselves "the best terrorists in the world," I would have to become a mock terrorist myself (my cover story was that I was an Al Jazeera reporter covering the insurgency), and do my best to keep up with the 350 509ers comprising the OPFOR in the current training exercise.

I was there to do a job, to record what was going on from a historian's perspective. My goal was to get as close to the action as possible, but fade into the woodwork and not interfere with the operations. I managed to stay close to the action and record the 509th's oral histories as they unfolded. This is the same technique I used in Iraq. I also surprised Griffith and I survived the entire exercise (the 509th lost 75% of their numbers during the exercise and my entire team was wiped out in an ambush).

About a month after training at Polk, I formally requested permission to join the 509th in Iraq in October and November. I had a hunch that the war would come to a head in November. The U.S. could not wait much longer to address the intolerable situation in Fallujah, where the terrorists had established a stronghold and operated with impunity. Fallujah had to be liberated.

I felt Fallujah would be the tipping point of the war, but wrongly assumed that the 509th, as one of the Army's premier urban warfare units, would participate in the inevitable assault on the city. Colonel Griffith, a bit surprised at the timing of my trip, asked if I was "an adrenaline junkie." I responded that I wanted to be there while history was being made, rather than read about it and interview his men after the fact. With no book deal, sponsor, and very little money in my bank account, I paid my one way to Iraq on October 12, 2004. (Four days earlier, my wife filed for divorce. Later, I would put my entire savings on the line to write this book.) I spent about three weeks with the 509th in Baghdad, raiding houses, inserting special operations teams, searching cars, barely avoiding IEDs, and talking to Iraqi civilians. Then I joined a Marine special ops unit, and finally a Marine infantry battalion (I was in Iraq for about three months).

I spent the entire time in uniform, mainly to blend in, to share the misery of the troopers, and later, in Fallujah, to avoid becoming a victim of friendly fire. Most of the terrorists were wearing civilian clothes. I was attached to front line rifle squads, the small teams which are actively waging the war in Iraq, to be as close to the action as possible.

I lived with the squads, patrolled with them, and helped do simple things when they were short of bodies. For the first time it's ever been done that I'm aware of, I also gathered their oral histories on a real-time basis, on combat missions. My goal was to capture the war from the perspective of the men in the squads and platoons fighting it. The only way to do it was to be in their boots and record the events as they occurred.

Not long after I joined the 509th, I interviewed the commander of the 2nd Brigade, 10th Mountain Division (the unit the 509th was assigned to). The colonel, a fellow historian at heart, bluntly asserted that "Fallujah will be the Gettysburg of this war." The battle was a potential turning point in history, and I wanted to be there. Also, because urban warfare is the deadliest form of combat, I knew the battle would prove or disprove my thesis that this is the "next greatest generation."

After arriving in Fallujah in early November, I was initially assigned to the Marine 2nd Recon Battalion, and accompanied missions searching for weapons of mass destruction, or setting up observation posts behind mujahideen lines. From a historian's perspective, this unique vantage point offered a panoramic view of the battle raging in the city.

With 2nd Recon, I had my first brushes with death. On two separate occasions, RPG rockets barely missed the Humvee I was riding in. In the second incident, the RPG blew up directly in front of me, blasting a huge ball of clay into our unarmored Humvee. The clay landed right in my gear.

A day before the battle, I was saved for the first time by a "presence" or a guardian angel I can't explain. Six Marines and I got caught in the open, and had to run and crawl for 500 meters under the fire of two snipers. I learned firsthand the difference between bullets whizzing past you and bullets that "snap," or literally miss you by inches. I was on my knees, crawling like mad, when the "presence" suddenly told me not to go any further. I ducked, an instant before a bullet snapped right past my head and landed where I was about to crawl next.

An hour after the sniper incident, I was about to settle down on a tree stump when I felt, "don't sit on the stump." I moved into a roofless building a few feet away. Seconds later the tree stump was obliterated by a mortar shell. Several Iraqi special forces troops were hit by shrapnel.

The whole time, I was never afraid of dying. In fact, I felt more alive in the city than ever before. I've never considered myself religious, but the presence I felt reaffirmed my faith. It's a feeling I hope I experience again before I pass from this world.

I was saved again by God's grace on the following day, when a Hellfire missile fell short of its target and vaporized the building in front of me. I remember laughing with the Marines and saying, "I think there was a building there." With the risk posed by friendly fire increasing by the hour, 2nd Recon withdrew the observation post on the third day of the battle.

My intent from the beginning was to accompany the men executing the main assault on the city, so when 2nd Recon pulled out, I requested permission to join one of the assault battalions. To my surprise, there was no shortage of embedded slots. Most the reporters assigned to the assault units bugged out and returned to headquarters as soon as the battle started.

I hitched a ride in a seven-ton truck bringing fresh reinforcements into the city. After a bumpy ride that lasted about a half an hour, I arrived at Fallujah's train station, and met the Marines of Lima Company, 3rd Battalion, 1st Marines (3/1). Lima Company was enjoying 24 hours of rest after enduring more than five days of heavy combat. Most of the men looked like the veterans from the battle of Iwo Jima. They all had the "thousand-yard stare," the outward manifestation of extreme physical exhaustion and prolonged, intense stress.

Lima Company had been tested severely, more so than any other unit I met. Almost from the beginning of the fight, Lima Company had received no support from tanks, air power, bulldozers, or any of America's advanced combat technologies. The men had been forced to fight like their WWII forebears, using rifles, grenades, and satchel charges to clear bunkers and houses. Their honor, commitment to each other, and shared adversity bonded them into a true family.

After a few minutes in the train station with Lima Company, I knew I had to remain with them for the duration of the battle. During the next several days I witnessed stunning bravery and courage under fire, memories I will carry for the rest of my life. Even after the platoon lost over 70% of its men, the Marines never complained. Some hid their wounds so they could remain with their buddies during the battle. The men of Lima Company fought with honor and for their brothers. The individuals I met in Iraq, especially in the Marines of 1st Platoon, showed me clearly that they truly do constitute the next Greatest Generation. Make no mistake about it; America's best is in Iraq.

After surviving the battle, I made an oath, a blood oath, that I would tell their story.

Chronology—1st Platoon
and the Battle of Fallujah

October 2002   Al-Qaeda ambushes Lima Company's 1st Platoon (part of Third Battalion, First Marines [3/1]) while they were training on Kuwait's Failaka Island. Lance Corporal (posthumously promoted Corporal) Antonio Sledd is killed by the terrorists.

March through   Operation Iraqi Freedom I culminates in the
May 2003   fall of Baghdad and Saddam Hussein's government. Lima Company conducts occupation duty in Sadr City.

June 2003   First Platoon returns to the United States from Operation Iraqi Freedom I. "Phase One" of the battle of Fallajah begins as former regime elements and terrorists attack American forces and use Fallujah as a sanctuary.

March 2004   The "new" 1st Platoon is formed after the platoon receives the "boot drop." First Platoon's NCOs are initially Hanks and Sojda. "Phase Two" of the battle of Fallujah begins with the death and mutilation of four American contractors in the heart of the city. The city continues to grow as the heart of the insurgency.

| April through May 2004 | The Marines are ordered to seize Fallujah. For six weeks the Marines conduct siege-type warfare and take a large portion of the city, but the operation is cancelled due to international outrage, based largely on biased or inaccurate television reporting. |

| June through October 2004 | First Platoon returns to Iraq. "Phase Three" of the battle begins as former Iraqi generals try to restore order inside the city. Abu Musab al-Zarqawi establishes his base inside Fallujah, creates bomb-making factories, and dispatches suicide bombers throughout Iraq. Hundreds of foreign fighters and international terrorists flock to the city. |

| November through December 2004 | Marines seize Fallujah and encounter some of the toughest urban combat since WWII and Hue City. 3/1 and 1st Platoon lead the Marine assault into the city; they have to clear the heart of Fallujah's defenses and a nest of international terrorism in Fallujah's Jolan district. |

| January 2005 | The city is clear of fighters, and residents of a Fallajah return to what's left of their homes. First Platoon returns to the United States, and Iraq holds its first free elections. |

| September 2005 | First Platoon returns to Iraq on the Syrian border to proudly serve their country. Not a single Marine in Lima Company fails to report for duty. |

Where They Are Now*

Corporal Adel Abudayeh—Recovered from his wounds and was promoted to Sergeant. He then moved to mainside before this most recent deployment. He was planning to get out, but he is now trying to come back to 3/1.

Lance Corporal Bradley Adams—Serving on the Iraqi-Syrian border.

Corporal Mario Alavez—Serving his third tour, along the Syrian border, promoted to squad leader.

Lance Corporal Donald Baker—Serving on the Iraqi-Syrian border.

Lance Corporal Roberto Barrickman—Serving on the Iraqi-Syrian border.

Staff Sergeant Steven "Pyro" Bodek—Retired from the Marine Corps, now serving in law enforcement.

*As of March 2006.

Lance Corporal Andrew Brockdorf—Serving on the Iraqi-Syrian border.

Sergeant Isidro Carreno—Recovered from his wounds and is now serving in 1/6 in Camp Lejeune.

Sergeant James "Bennie" Conner—Transferred out of Lima Company to cadre a new Marine regiment. He specifically joined the unit for the opportunity to return to serve his country by completing his fourth combat tour. Conner was awarded the Navy Commendation Medal (with valor) for his actions in Fallujah.

Lance Corporal Frank Contreras—Serving on the Iraqi-Syrian border.

Lance Corporal Jackie Damico—Serving on the Iraqi-Syrian border.

Lance Corporal Jacob de la Garza—Serving on the Iraqi-Syrian border.

Gunnery Sergeant Mathew Hackett—Serving as a Marine instructor in New York.

Major Brian Heatherman—Promoted to major, serving at Camp Pendleton, CA.

Corporal Micah Huyett—Recovered from his wounds, now serving on the Iraqi-Syrian border.

Corporal "Jack Rabbit"—Discharged from the Marine Corps Reserves and now gainfully employed.

Lance Corporal James—Serving on the Iraqi-Syrian border.

Lance Corporal Marshall Kennedy—Serving on the Iraqi-Syrian border.

Lance Corporal Heath Kramer—Retired from the Corps, gainfully employed, and awarded the Bronze Star with V for his actions in Fallujah.

Staff Sergeant Jason Kyle—Promoted to Staff Sergeant, 1st Platoon, serving along the Iraqi-Syrian border.

Lance Corporal Derick Lowe—Combat wounded in Iraq along the Iraqi-Syrian border during his second tour of duty.

Corporal Kevin Myirski—Promoted to Sergeant, then moved to Security Forces in D.C.

Corporal Darren Paul—Transferred to Weapon Training Battalion in Quantico.

Lance Corporal Giovanni Perez—Serving on the Iraqi-Syrian border.

Lance Corporal Philip Peterson—Serving on the Iraqi-Syrian border.

Sergeant Shawn Pourier—Recovered from his wounds, now serving on the Iraqi-Syrian border.

Sergeant Todd "Slaughter" Rosalez—After being hospitalized for back injuries that nearly ended his career, Rosalez requested and received permission to return to Iraq. Sergeant Rosalez transferred to 1/4 and is deployed in Iraq/Kuwait.

Lance Corporal Dean Scott—Serving on the Iraqi-Syrian border.

Sergeant Greg Smith—After nearly dying of his wounds, Smith is now Lima's stateside representative. It took Congressional intervention for him to receive even the most minimal compensation from the Veteran's Administration.

Corporal Bill Sojda—Completed his tour in the Marine Corps and is now seeking a career in law enforcement. A true patriot, Sojda reflected: "I'd do it all again, even if I knew the outcome."

First Lieutenant Jeff Sommers—Promoted to first lieutenant and deployed as CAAT (Combined Anti-Armor Team) Platoon Commander, serving on the Iraqi-Syrian border.

Private Andrew Sean Stokes—Serving in Iraq along the Syrian border. The Marine Corps has yet to promote Stokes, yet he still leads the way in Iraq.

Lance Corporal Peter Suguitan—Serving on the Iraqi-Syrian border.

Corporal David Taptto—Recovered from his wounds. Promoted to sergeant and discharged from the Marine Corps.

Hospitalman "Doc" Tovar—Serving on the Iraqi-Syrian border.

Sergeant Daniel Tremore—Transferred to 1st Platoon as platoon sergeant, and now serving on the Iraqi-Syrian border.

Lance Corporal Dustin Turpen—Serving on the Iraqi-Syrian border.

Lance Corporal Chris Vales—Serving on the Iraqi-Syrian border.

Staff Sergeant Michael S. Van Daele—Awarded the Bronze Star with V, and moved to School of Infantry when we got back from Fallujah.

Lance Corporal Steven Wade—Serving on the Iraqi-Syrian border.

Gunnery Sergeant David Wilson—Serving at Camp Pendleton, California.

Corporal Toya Yin—After recovering from wounds, Yin was honorably discharged from the Marine Corps.

Notes

I conducted scores of oral history interviews with Marines, Iraqi soldiers, and civilians. Many of the interviews were conducted during the battle of Fallujah in November 2004. To the best of my knowledge, the way I gathered the material is a first for a historian. I realized that to capture the story you have to be there. I noticed that so many members of this generation, like the WWII generation, tried to bury the war after they came home. They rarely talked about their combat experiences in Iraq to outsiders who were not there. After I came home from Fallujah, I found myself trying to bury the war, it was a painful experience. Initially, I decided not to write this book but the parents of the men encouraged me, so people would understand what their sons went through.

Most experts agree that Iraq is a squad and platoon-level war. The official documents and reporting rarely seems to probe into this micro-level view of the war. Oral history is one way to tell this "grunt" level view of the war. Every interview in this book was painstakingly corroborated by other interviews and multiple sources. Nevertheless, faulty memories (a low risk since the oral histories were largely recorded as the battle was occurring) and skewed perspectives are all inherent dangers with oral history. At times the individual memories did not jibe with the collective memory. These same flaws are also found in the documentary record. Nevertheless, the sources, methodology, and the documents confirm the historical accuracy of the events told in this book.

Oral history interviews were obtained whenever we had time to break, or when the company and the platoon went firm for the night. The stories of most of 1st Platoon's significant actions were corroborated through group interviews. While their memories were still fresh, I spent several hundred hours reconstructing every aspect of their battle. Furthermore, 3/1's historian gave me access to unit documents, the entire Command Chronologies, and maps that detailed the platoon and battalion's story before and during the battle. This documentation was used to corroborate the oral material. Many senior Marine officers close to the planning, command, and execution of the battle also freely gave me their time and input. Unless otherwise noted, all dialogue and narrative in this book comes from corroborated oral history interviews which have been vetted. This is their story, in their own words.

Chapter 2. A Grunt's Grunt

page 22: "G/3/1's superior service in the face of intense, prolonged combat operations in Korea. Shall be carried into combat again, for service in Iraqi Operation Freedom II." 3/1 Battalion Command Chronology, January 1 to June 30, 2004.

Chapter 4. Trojan Horses

page 43: "One of the worst attacks occurred on September the 14th . . ." 3/1 Battalion Command Chronology, September 1 to September 30, 2004.

page 46: "By men believed to have been led by one of the battalion's previous fired interpreters." Delta's commanding officer and his brother were tied to the Mujahideen. 3/1 Battalion Command Chronology, September 1 to September 30, 2004.

page 46: "Deter and disrupt . . ." 3/1 Battalion Command Chronology, September 1 to September 30, 2004.

page 46: "Designed to deceive the enemy . . ." 3/1 Battalion Command Chronology, September 1 to September 30, 2004.

Chapter 5. Feints

page 50: "The enemy, at this point, was fully established and operating in the safe haven of Fallujah . . ." 3/1 Battalion Command Chronology, October 1, 2004 to October 30, 2004.

page 51: "Fallujah's 39,000 buildings . . ." Interview with Lieutenant Colonel Scott Shuster.

page 52: "15,000 displaced civilians . . ." Interview with Lieutenant Colonel Scott Shuster.

Chapter 6. The Die Is Cast

pages 74–75: MICLIC details gathered from Staff Sergeant S. Bodek during Marine combat engineer interview.

CHAPTER 7. "I'm Gonna Take You to Hell"

page 81: "A typical Fallujah city block was about 100 × 200 meters long . . ." Operation Al-Fajr debrief prepared for RCT-1.

CHAPTER 9. "Allahu Akbar"

pages 104–5: Jihadi cell phone conversation publicly available: Gunnery Sergeant David Wilson.

CHAPTER 10. Back into the Fray

page 128: "[Van Daele] courageously arose from his cover position, exposing himself to direct fire." Summary of action in citation for Bronze Star with Combat Valor awarded to Staff Sergeant Michael Van Daele.

CHAPTER 11. A Whiter Shade of Pale

Details on unit action come from 3/1 Battalion Command Chronology, November 1 to November 30, 2004.

CHAPTER 12. "So Far Together"

All dialogue and narrative from oral history interviews obtained by the author.

page 145: "They continuously encounter pockets of determined resistance." 3/1 Battalion Command Chronology, November 1 to November 30, 2004.

CHAPTER 13. Full Circle

page 160: "Suguitan's two-man rocket team made its way to the roof . . ." Several shots from the sniper ricocheted and almost hit me. Because they were so short on personnel, I eventually helped clear some buildings, while doing my primary job of recording their story, a practice I maintained through the battle. My main task was recording oral histories during breaks in the fighting, a first of its kind. I also carried a tiny video recorder and captured most of 1st Platoon's battle on video tape, as long as the batteries held out.

page 164: "The battalion air officer orchestrated attacks on twenty-four targets . . ." 3/1 Battalion Command Chronology, 1 November 2004 to 30 November 2004.

CHAPTER 14. The Wolves of Islam

page 168: "A Che Guevera-like one-legged terrorist . . ." Paul J. Murphy, *The Wolves of Islam* (Dulles, VA: Brassey's, 2004), p. 74.

page 169: Post-battle intelligence on Chechen activities obtained by the author through interviews with senior Marine Corps officers.

CHAPTER 15. D9s

page 186: "Some people snapped after Hanks was killed . . ." For me, I realized that nothing can prepare you for the feeling you have after dragging the lifeless body of a fellow American. From the experience, I grew to understand the need to survive at all costs and the initial visceral instinct for vengeance. The Marines in Iraq keep their emotions inside and fight on with honor.

page 190: "It doesn't happen enough, but I want to thank you for your service here." Author witnessed ceremony and conversation during the battle.

CHAPTER 17. Requiem

The author also mourned the loss of the fallen Marines, and was the sole recorder of the ceremony. All the feelings we buried from the battle seemed to come back that day.

Index

ACKNOWLEDGMENTS

I AM INDEBTED TO THE HUNDREDS OF MARINES AND SOLDIERS who shared their battlefield oral histories with me while I was in Iraq. They told me their stories, not to honor themselves, but to honor their fallen comrades. In particular, I would like to thank all of the troopers in the 509th Parachute (the first unit with whom I was embedded), and the Marines of the 2nd Recon Battalion and Lima Company of the 3rd Battalion, 1st Marines. I am grateful especially to Lieutenant Jeff Sommers, Sergeant James Conner, and Corporal Bill Sojda for reading the draft manuscript and going through many follow-up interviews. This was a painful process for them since it involved going back in time and reliving the battle.

I am grateful to my friends and family who stood by my side during the months I spent in Iraq. I am extremely thankful to my daughter Lily and my parents for always being there for me. Additionally, I am extremely grateful to my agent, Andy Zack of the Zack Company, for always believing in me and my quest to gather the oral histories of our troops. I'd like to thank my friend Carl Fornaris, who encouraged me while I was in Iraq and safeguarded my emailed descriptions of my experiences. Most important, I thank my close friend, Brian Fitzpatrick, whose ideas, inspiration, and edits to the book proved invaluable; his help and advice are a crucial part of this book. I am also extremely grateful to my editor,

Robert Pigeon, who championed this project and encouraged me throughout the entire process. Our association seemed like fate since Bob was the perfect editor for this book.

Additionally, I am grateful to Major David Tippett, Lieutenant Colonel Farlow, and Major Joe Edstrom for caring about my welfare. Major Web Wright went the extra mile and somehow got me to Fallujah. I would also like to thank Lieutenant Colonel Dan "Mad Max" Griffith, the commanding officer of the 509th Parachute and "insurgent leader" at Fort Polk, for encouraging me in the early stages of this project. Additionally, I am grateful to Navy Captain Michael Franken, my former neighbor, who first gave me the idea to go to Iraq, and Jay Chambers, who was the first to mention to me the idea of the next "Greatest Generation." I would also like to thank Colonel Michael Shupp and Lieutenant Colonel Buhl for helping in numerous ways. Additionally, I am thankful to 3/1's historian, Captain "Puc" Gulluglio. I am especially grateful to my friend, Marine Rajai Hakki, whom I met shortly after the battle of Fallujah. Rajai carefully looked over the Arabic translations in the book and gave good editorial advice. Like so many Arab-Americans, he has sacrificed a great deal for his country. Shortly after 9/11, in a spirit of patriotism, he dropped out of college and joined the Corps. His tour of duty in Iraq culminated with the siege of Fallujah, where his well-honed skills in Iraqi dialect were used in enemy interrogations as part a Human Exploitation Team (HET).

Finally, I would like to thank the families of the fallen Marines for their cooperation. Your sons, your husbands, your fathers—they are heroes. Many of the stories in this book will bring back painful memories—for that I am truly sorry. But I sincerely hope that in the retelling, I have paid proper tribute to the heroic and unselfish sacrifices of these Marines, the next "Greatest Generation," and told their story with honor. They deserve nothing less.